'Nigel's story speaks powerfully [...] Weaving together tales from his a[...] and spiritual insights, *Stories from [...]* faith-affirming read, which encour[...] hand at work in every area and chapter of life, just as Nigel does.'
Rt Reverend Saju Muthalaly, Bishop of Loughborough

'It was my privilege to ordain Nigel in 2018. But Nigel is no ordinary priest. His trusty Harley-Davidson has taken him all around the world as a member (and President) of the God's Squad. *Stories from the Road* is an honest, humorous and at times scary account of how God has inspired, guided and protected him on his journeys. His faith shines through like a light in the darkness.'
Rt Rev Martyn Snow, Bishop of Leicester

'In a down-to-earth, honest and sometimes humorous manner, this long-time biker and more recent Anglican priest takes you along for the ride. His own eccentricity, stubbornness and resilience sit alongside unexpected provision, grace and warmth that reflect on a lifetime of devotion, to both motorcycles and Christ. A heartwarming read.'
Sean Stillman, author God's Biker: Motorcycles & Misfits

... of the God of surprises.
... his adventures on his motorbike
... is an uplifting and
... hopes us all to look for God's
... Mind

Stories from the Road

Observations from the Saddle of an Ageing Harley

Rev Nigel Rostock

instant apostle

First published in Great Britain in 2024

Instant Apostle
104A The Drive
Rickmansworth
Herts
WD3 4DU

British Library Cataloguing-in-Publication Data

A catalogue record for this book is available from the British Library.

This book and all other Instant Apostle books are available from Instant Apostle:

Website: www.instantapostle.com

Email: info@instantapostle.com

ISBN 978-1-912726-80-6

Printed in Great Britain.

This book is dedicated to my loving wife, Alison.

My best friend and faithful travelling companion,
on the road and on our shared journey through life.

An encouragement to carry on, a challenge to do better,
and a life lived fully for her Saviour.

Contents

Introduction

For more than fifteen years now, I have been drawing inspiration from my many journeys on my cherished Harley Davidson. All in all, this ageing bike has taken me more than 160,000 miles. It has carried me across Alps, through snow-covered moors and along the steep incline approaching the summit of an Italian volcano. All of these stories are authentic accounts of some of these journeys, with reflections inspired along the way.

As a member of a Christian motorcycle club and an Anglican vicar, you might imagine that I would make faith connections, and you would be right. So I hope you enjoy reading these accounts as much as I have enjoyed living them.

In taking these journeys, there have also been highly significant sections of the ride, as well as noteworthy breaks and experiences on the way, which have had enormous and lasting impact. The lessons that informed my future journeys were important, drawing on these experiences, both positive and negative. Furthermore, there were aspects of the journeys where God intervened, sometimes in obvious and powerful ways, where if He had not, the journey would have concluded abruptly, and with clear finality. Similarly, my own faith journey has held significant moments along the way, as well as clear forks in the road leading in diametrically opposed directions. Some of these were roads leading to potentially magnificent mountaintop experiences, while the opposite were leading down potentially devastating avenues. Here, I will begin by sharing some of these significant moments on my own journey through faith. Therefore, in order to appreciate the way God has moved in my life, it will be important to first share a little of my own background and story.

Part One
A Journey into Faith

1

Not the Best Way to Enter the World

I actually began life in a hospital in Leigh in Greater Manchester on a cold January morning in 1964, having apparently been conceived as the result of a forced sexual encounter, which my biological mother later related to me when I finally made contact. Although she already had a son slightly older than me, she was prevented from bringing me home by my biological grandmother, whom she was living with, not least owing to the circumstance of my conception. Even then, I believe, God was looking after me, and I realise that if this had not been the case, I would probably never have seen the light of day.

Having been abandoned at the hospital, it wasn't long before I was collected and taken to another home in Manchester, where I was subsequently adopted by a decent, down-to-earth, working-class couple, whom I always recognised as my actual parents. This has been a helpful analogy for me, when I have grappled with the way we can truly be sons of God.[1] Being adopted by God the Father into sonship is as real a relationship and reality as my own adoption by my own earthly parents. I realise that not all parents, mothers or fathers, have been positive influences, and it can be difficult equating divine Fatherhood in these circumstances.

I finally met my biological father much later in life, several years before he died, and not knowing what to expect. My half-sister had related to me, the first time we met, how she had gone

---

[1] Romans 8:14-15.

out with a boy her father didn't like. When he came to pick her up, she told me that her father had gone for him with an axe, which lodged in the roof of the car as he ducked in the driving seat. They then sped off with this axe embedded in the roof. Unsurprisingly, the relationship with the boy didn't last. This in part explained my own unpredictable nature, which I had obviously inherited, and which accompanied a more placid nature that had developed from my upbringing.

It is important to recognise, though, that God the Father is perfect, lacking the negative traits of our own parents, and He may even be the first real loving Father we experience. This adoption is nonetheless as real as the adoption by the couple who welcomed me into their home and brought me up.

On Sundays in the early 1970s, not dissimilar to many other couples in those days, my parents would take part in two central activities. My father would spend hours washing and polishing our Ford Cortina on the driveway, while my mother would drag me to a local Church of England service. The church was located in the middle of a rough, deprived council estate, which one of my then closest friends also lived on. I could share some interesting stories of what we got up to there, and most of which I sometimes criticise in others, until my wife annoyingly points out, 'Didn't you do that when you were younger?'

The church was very traditional, and while I went through the motions, I had no real understanding of who God was. It is possible to do this all our lives, following what are in essence empty rituals and practices, until we come into a real relationship with Jesus.[2]

---

[2] The Pharisees of Jesus' time, who were the religious leaders, were a little like this, focusing on the ritual at the expense of the relationship – see Matthew 23:23.

2
Early Days

In the 1970s, besides attending church, it was certainly colourful growing up, living in a cul-de-sac which had both a piggery and an orchard at the end of the road. Having no adopted siblings, I would spend a great deal of time with my friends, who also lived in this cul-de-sac. We used to climb over the wall of the orchard and sit chatting, catching the grasshoppers which covered the wooden, creosoted fence surrounding the outer edges of the orchard, or scrumping a few apples, before often being chased and shot at with pellets by the owner. We were of course banned from trespassing in the orchard, and would come home to big trouble if our parents found out about it. Those times were special, though; we often don't appreciate those simple pleasures until they are gone. While the orchard held special memories, the piggery became legendary.

It was a day just like any other, with the sun blazing down on a peaceful midsummer Sunday afternoon. Suddenly, this peace was exploded with the sound of the patter of tiny feet. As I peered through the multicoloured venetian blinds which hung from my parents' lounge window, a sea of small pink noses was gathering at the end of the road. From an initial patter of tiny feet, a whole herd of pigs stampeded past our lounge window. There was a deafening sound of high-pitched squeals like the sound of screeching tyres spinning out of control, with tiny legs motoring down the avenue, and their small curly tails following. I have never seen a more amusing sight since, with the owner and his two sons giving chase with little chance of stopping them. The whole herd disappeared around the corner, onto the estate. One of my friends had been the culprit – he had talked about how amusing it would be to let the pigs out, but I didn't think he would actually go through with it. It wasn't long after this that he predictably ended up in the local Borstal, or Youth Detention Centre.

Looking back at this episode, I can't help thinking about the story of Jesus in Luke 8:26-39, driving out a legion of demons from a man who lived, tormented and afflicted among the graves. Here, Jesus set the man free, and after the demons pleaded with Jesus not to destroy them, they were sent into a herd of pigs. The demon-infested pigs then careered down towards some water, before drowning, and leaving the man in his right mind. Those looking after the herd appeared to care little for the healed man, and seemed more concerned about the pigs, as the people, now full of fear then turned on Jesus, pleading with Him to leave. I can imagine those responsible for the herd running after these pigs as they headed off towards the water, just like the ones that filled my road on their own bid for freedom.

These early days were carefree, without the distraction of mobile phones, computer screens or video games. This was a time when the black-and-white television consisted of two channels. What this meant was that we had to invent our own amusement. We would meet in the middle of the street and organise simple games of British Bulldog or Red Rover, or even talk about the recent moon landing. The summers seemed to go on forever in those early days, and much of my time was spent with friends, either exploring the nearby woods or searching for newts in the local brooks and ponds around the local golf links.

Throughout the 1970s, we spent a great deal of time at the local swimming pool, which also still contained a series of public baths. Although this sounds implausible in modern times, this was common during my childhood, particularly in my area, where many homes were without bathrooms; this was where families would come to take their weekly baths together. The swimming pool was also basic, cold and in need of refurbishment, and when the lights were first turned on, the floor would come alive as its mosaic-like tiles began to move, and teams of cockroaches scurried to find cover from the light. Yet we didn't seem to mind sharing this antiquated pool with this local wildlife.

After the summer of 1975, I attended a local comprehensive school in Eccles. For me, school was just as carefree, mainly because I often refused to do the work, preferring to mess around or just daydream during lessons. Religion was interwoven into the fabric of the school day, which always began with an assembly, consisting of several hymns and prayers. I did enjoy my schooldays, though, spending untroubled hours with friends – with low expectations from teachers who had given up on me and held little hope that I would take anything seriously.

I also found myself in a tiny bit of trouble with the police while at school and, predictably, I eventually left with appalling grades, in addition to an inability to understand or use basic punctuation. The teachers advised that I had gone as far as I could academically, which was nowhere! However, it gave me great pleasure in later life to complete two theological degrees and write a PhD thesis, before ironically becoming a teacher.

The truth was that the trajectory of my life was heading for disaster during these early days, and it was purely down to a life-changing encounter with Jesus that I was turned around. This gives me great encouragement, having experienced being written off myself, that God can change any situation or any life. One of my school reports said, 'Nigel has the capacity to ask the most ridiculous questions in class.' I take that as a compliment, because what others perceive as ridiculous might just be the question that needs asking. God doesn't write any of us off, and I know if He could help me, He can certainly help anyone.

On leaving school in 1980, I had the compulsory meeting with the careers officer. He asked me, 'What do you want to do next?' I told him I had not got a clue. He said, 'Name some jobs.'

I really hadn't given my future any thought, let alone what job I wanted to do. All I could think of was a half-remembered nursery rhyme, so I replied, 'Butcher, baker, candlestick maker,' and just before I had chance to repeat 'beggar man, thief', he stopped me.

'What made you say baker?'

I couldn't say it was part of the rhyme that had popped into my head, and before I had a chance to come up with a rationale, he told me there was a bakery course at Salford Technical College, now Salford University, which he enrolled me on to. This led to a job at a bakery, which lasted six months.

I was responsible for making the bread at night, which would be shipped out to the numerous bakeries around Salford. One particular night I forgot the salt. The salt does two things – it stops the yeast from excessively rising and it gives the bread taste. So the bread started to rise very successfully, but it didn't stop rising, until it was the tallest bread you have ever seen. I had to make a decision then either to tell someone or to risk sending the bread out. I sent it out.

Not only was the bread very tall, it was also very tasteless. So all the bread was sent back from around Salford, and I was in the office with my short-lived bakery career in tatters. It was, however, a few weeks before I let my parents know, and I continued to get up and ride into town, making out that I was going to work.

Ironically, losing this job was the best thing that could have happened to me, as it led to me escaping in the summer of 1984 to work at a holiday camp in Morecambe, where I was to meet my wife a year later.

I actually arrived at the holiday camp in my run-down Ford Capri, which expired not long after arriving. It was early in the evening when I drove, with three friends, a little too fast around a particularly tight, unfamiliar bend. The narrow lane curved to the right, but we continued straight on. The car left the ground like a scene from a movie and landed in a field. My three friends left their seats and hit their heads sharply on the roof. The engine was now full of turf from the field and was smoking badly, as the turf had destroyed the radiator.

We removed the remainder of the grass from the engine and managed to drive the car back to the holiday camp, smoking and overheating, where it remained until the end of the season.

Having killed the car, I eventually decided to buy a motorcycle from a local bike shop in Morecambe. This was when my passion for riding really took off. I bought a relatively fast two-stroke Japanese bike. I loved the freedom of riding around the local villages, weaving through the tight narrow bends or riding along the coastal roads. I would ride in all weathers, often travelling between Morecambe and Manchester at weekends as I visited my home, with only a T-shirt and leather jacket to protect me from the elements. It was also useful, after eventually meeting Alison, to be able to take her out to the local pubs in Morecambe and Lancaster, and to be able to escape the confines of the holiday camp.

3
Finding Hope, Finding Jesus

The holiday camp understandably no longer exists in Morecambe, and after plans to turn it into a prison failed, the site was converted into a gated community. The camp overlooked a slightly brown-tinted sea, with views of the nuclear power plant from the beach. At that time, many of the workers were escaping their pasts, and it was a little like a holiday-themed version of the French Foreign Legion. The reality, though, was that it was a soulless, deprived and hopeless place, when you scratched the surface. Still, it was here that, in 1985, I met Alison, the woman who would shortly become my wife, and it was here that she asked me to take her to a Billy Graham meeting, which was being held at the Sheffield football stadium.

I really had no interest in Christianity, and didn't particularly like Christians at that point, but I agreed to go. I had decided that if I had to be there, then I would at least pick up a friend, along with his girlfriend, on the way. It was actually a bit of a trek to Sheffield: catching a bus to Lancaster followed by a train to Manchester, where we would borrow my dad's car to take us to Sheffield.

We arrived at the football stadium. I had an unexplainable compulsion which drew me to that place. There was no logical rationale for this, as when we set out I had no real desire to be there. In fact, I would much rather have visited a local pub. However, now it felt as though there was something almost compelling me to be there.

The four of us exited the car and made our way to the stands overlooking the football stadium. There was a small stage on the pitch, with an organ playing corny old music. Next, the famous American evangelist, Billy Graham, appeared and began to speak. It wasn't a spectacular speech as such, as he talked about the need to repent, telling us that there was a judgement to be faced, that we had all sinned and that we were all guilty. I certainly knew I was guilty as I contemplated a road traffic hearing that was impending, as well as a string of things I had been in trouble for as a teenager. Normally, I might have objected or just walked out, but I felt a real conviction.

We don't often hear preaching like this nowadays, but the Bible is certainly clear on this starting point. Until we appreciate our predicament, we are unlikely to see a need for a solution. This, in fact, was his following point. Billy Graham continued that there was a solution to this impending judgement, to the sin that puts us into this predicament, separating us from God. The solution, Billy Graham suggested, was Jesus. He went on to explain how much God loves us, that Jesus was willing to die to set us free, to pay the penalty Himself. This was why Jesus came, why He died on the cross, to take the punishment we deserved, to pay for our sins on this same cross, to allow us to be in relationship with Him.

Billy Graham finally talked about repentance, the need for sincere regret, being sorry for the things we have done. He also talked about the need to accept Jesus' sacrifice, to do something about it, to follow Jesus. As he explained, this wasn't a type of servitude, it wasn't oppressive, but something that brought freedom.

After giving this talk, he then gave an altar call, which again is not as common today, but was an opportunity to go forward as an act of faith that a decision had been made to follow Jesus. I felt a compulsion to go forward, almost like being drawn by a magnet. I looked at Alison, who was also now on her feet, feeling this same compulsion. It was like St Paul on the road to Damascus, where he recognised Jesus speaking to him on the road. God caused him to be temporarily blind, and after three days, physical scales fell from his eyes, enabling him to see not only the world but seeing the spiritual reality of who Jesus really was. This is why we call a life-changing enlightenment a Damascus Road experience.[3] This is what this was; it was as though everything made sense, and Alison felt exactly the same way. We made our way forward, someone prayed for us, we were given a copy of the Gospels, and we returned to our seats feeling noticeably changed.

My friend and his girlfriend had been exposed to exactly the same experience but remained unmoved. I have since understood that this transformation is the work of the Holy Spirit, the third person of the Trinity,[4] who allows us to see the reality of the world and the reality of who Jesus is and draws us into an authentic relationship with Him. In fact, we can only recognise 'the Father, Son, and Spirit in terms of eternal relations'.[5]

This reality we experienced was a far cry from the empty ritual I had previously known. In fact, it is this relationship that allows us to follow traditional liturgies, but with a reality and authenticity in what we do.

We left that stadium completely transformed. There was a real joy and excitement in our souls; there was a tangible sense of peace, a sense of freedom.

The next morning, we woke up and headed off to work, and the world had literally changed. The trees were almost technicoloured, the world looked bright, almost intense, as if

---

[3] Acts 9:1-19.

[4] 'The Holy Trinity' is a term used for the Christian belief in one God in three persons. The three divine persons are identified in the Bible as God the Father, God the Son (Jesus) and God the Holy Spirit.

[5] Nigel Rostock, 'Two Different Gods or Two Types of Unity? A Critical Response to Zizioulas' Presentation of "The Father as Cause" with Reference to the Cappadocian Fathers and Augustine', *New Blackfriars: A Review*, 2010, p 331.

someone had swapped a black-and-white television set for a flat screen, high-definition, coloured version. There was an intense feeling of love for God in our hearts. In addition, there was also the realisation that we couldn't remain at the holiday camp, now feeling the emptiness of the place. We decided to go grape-picking in France, intending to get a tent from Leicester on the way from Alison's house. I had also been able to rearrange the hearing for my traffic violation to be held in Leicester, before we finally headed off to France.

In fact, what actually happened was that we arrived at Leicester, became members of a local church, found jobs and got married just five months after meeting in late October 1985, in the exact church where I am now a vicar, now nearly forty years later. God certainly moves in mysterious ways!

4
New-found Faith

As I mentioned, I was due in court in Leicester, as the authorities had caught up with me over numerous motoring violations I had gained on the bike while living in Morecambe.

I had first come to the attention of the local police as I was taking Alison's friend into Morecambe town centre. I approached a set of traffic lights, gradually slowing down as they were on red. The lights turned green, I pulled back on the throttle, inadvertently lifted the bike onto its rear wheel, and rode across the junction with the front wheel in the air. While I began crossing the junction with a passenger, I completed the manoeuvre without her. As I lifted the bike onto its rear wheel, my passenger slid off into the path of a clean, white, shining vehicle, complete with its blue light and two police officers. They sat watching this unusual scene unfolding before their eyes, and fortunately they were now unable to follow me owing to Alison's friend lying in the road in front of them.

For a split second, I contemplated going straight back to pick her up, but decided better of it. I did notice in my mirror that she was climbing to her feet, and so I disappeared into the distance. I returned later to find the police car had left, and picked her up with lots of apologies. Ironically, this whole incident had made her day, and she wasn't at all injured. The problem was that the police had got a clear side view of me, and were understandably looking out for my bike.

I was subsequently pulled over several times after that, and on the final time, as I rode through a shopping precinct, the police were waiting for me on the other side. When these misdemeanours were added up, they equated to fifteen penalty points, and I had now been summoned. Fifteen points was a clear ban and I could sense that I was going to be forced to change my status from biker to pedestrian.

I entered the magistrates' court with little hope of a positive outcome. I was, however, praying during this hearing, but I have to admit with little faith that God could overturn this one. It was cut and dried. The question was asked, 'Do you admit to the charges brought against you?' I couldn't with a clear conscience deny them. The penalty was predictable, as they gave me fifteen points, a heavy fine and a ban. Unusually, a further question was asked: 'Is there any reason we shouldn't take your licence off you?'

I couldn't believe I was saying this, but I replied, 'I have just become a Christian, and I realise what I did was wrong, so won't be doing it again,' as if this would make a difference.

I really couldn't believe the next thing they said to me: 'We will give you fifteen points and you will be given a heavy fine, but we won't take your licence, after all.'

I had been praying, but didn't really believe I would be leaving with my licence! I have no doubt that God was responding to my prayers. This could almost have been a parable describing my recent conversion. I was guilty and knew it, I was sincerely repentant and, while there was a cost, I was set free, as God responded to my plea for help. It was certainly a talking point as I would show doubters my unique licence containing an unheard-of fifteen points printed on the back.

There was one other reason I wanted to stop off in Leicester, and this was in order to settle some unfinished business with someone. It was a situation that threatened to seriously change the whole course of our lives. Without going into detail, before my encounter with Jesus in Sheffield, I thought that peace could only come through getting even with people, and this was my intention, which would have had serious consequences. The difficult reality, though, was that, as a Christian, it was clear I could not go through with this course of action, and I needed to forgive the individual. This was easier said than done, and several times I grappled with these feelings, until God brought peace into my heart. I have since realised that forgiveness releases us from the chains that bind and torment us, and ultimately sets us free from bitterness, which only ever destroys.

Sometimes forgiveness also needs expressing – not all the time, but sometimes it is something we need to do to gain closure. For me this came about in a miraculous manner, shortly after arriving in Leicester in 1986. I was sitting at the dining table, eating my dinner with Alison, when God clearly spoke to me, telling me to get up, ride across town to where this guy lived and tell him I forgave him. It was as if I was again being compelled to do it at this exact moment.

I got up, leaving a half-eaten dinner, with Alison asking, 'What are you doing?'

I replied that God had told me to go round to this guy's flat and tell him I forgave him.

She said, 'Aren't you going to finish your dinner?', looking at me as though I was a little out of my mind.

I said, 'No, God has told me to go now.'

I got on my bike and rode across town to where he lived. I turned up at exactly the same moment that he arrived in a car. I had pulled up in his parking space, and he wasn't happy. I climbed off the bike, stepped over to his car, opened the door and climbed into the passenger seat. I told him what my intentions had been, but that I had become a Christian and that I needed to tell him I forgave him, and that the slate was clean as far as I was concerned. We disagreed on the possible outcome of the potential confrontation, but this drew a line under things. I still didn't like him, we would never be friends, but I was able to express my forgiveness.

Far from letting him off the hook, it was actually the other way around. Unforgiveness makes us prisoners and takes away our peace, and this act gave me freedom. The fact was that if I had turned up any other time, he would not have opened the door to me, let alone engaged in conversation. This was actually the only scenario which would have worked, but it needed exact timing. This is the reality of the way God works in our lives. He isn't passive; He speaks to us, guides us, whispers to us, and on odd occasions, as with this example, makes Himself heard in order to bring healing and peace into often troubled lives.

The impact of this new-found faith could not remain theoretical, and I developed a desire to get to know God better, to be able to live in the light of this transformation. In 1993 I began a theological course which gave a good grounding to the New Testament, and helped me understand the Bible better. The great theologian St Augustine (AD354-430) expressed the necessity of faith seeking understanding, and this was exactly what I was compelled to do.

This also created an interesting by-product: as I began to study the New Testament language of Greek, I began to gain a better grasp of the English language, recognising why punctuation was so important, something I had refused to grasp at school. Now, as I understood its purpose, I began to utilise it.

Having worked for a while in a laundry, at a swimming pool and in a lightbulb factory, finally in 1994 God clearly led me into working with those experiencing long-term homelessness and alcohol abuse. I had bumped into an old pastor acquaintance who had recommended visiting a hostel run by a fairly eccentric minister, with whom he had previously worked for a couple of years. This place was unique, rough and ready, but totally impolitically authentic. I gave this minister a call, asking if he had any vacancies.

To my surprise he replied, 'Come down and we will see how we get on, but I can't promise anything.' I was thinking this would be the most informal interview I have ever attended, and I said to myself, 'Of course you can't promise me anything, you haven't even met me yet!'

I arrived at a long row of interconnected terraced houses and was taken to a room at the front of the building. The minister entered the room and said, 'We do have a vacancy, but we may only be able to offer it for a week or two, and we don't allow alcohol in the building.' The penny now dropped: this wasn't an interview; it was an offer of lodgings.

After clearing this one up, we chatted and it appeared that they had actually been expecting God to lead someone to join them in the work, and discerned that it was me they had been waiting for.

This was only one of the many times I was mistaken for a resident. On one occasion, a middle-class lady brought some food for us and then proceeded to lecture me on why I was too young to be living there and why I needed to find a job. I had obviously fitted in too well.

I eventually spent ten years working with these old-school, hard-core drinkers within this unique long-term hostel where faith informed the way we interacted with these men. This was a real down-to-earth and raw environment, where men whom other hostels couldn't handle were recommended to us. Some of these men were extremely dangerous, others difficult, as were some of the volunteers who appeared from time to time. God was at work, though, being present in the conversations over cups of tea and within the confrontations as difficult men attempted to intimidate and manipulate, often after having been out drinking heavily.

However, in this place where intimidation didn't work and manipulation was clearly identified, these men's lives were transformed, and the community became a real expression of home and family as they began to care deeply for one another. In fact, I took my young son Luke along one day when I prepared and served something resembling porridge, which they were gracious enough to tolerate. As I came through into the rudimentary dining room, a notorious street fighter with hands twice the size of my own, who had previously killed a man in a pub fight and launched more than one can of beer at my own head in the past, was now sitting with my young son, stirring milk into his porridge with real care and gentleness. It was ruined slightly, though, as another notorious six-foot-two Polish brawler began to describe in vivid detail the shortcomings of my cooking skills to my son as he passed by.

It was here that the minister who ran this hostel suggested that I attend theological college on a full-time basis, and offered to support me. So, in 1996, I began to attend London Bible College and completed a theological degree before continuing on to complete a Master's degree in biblical interpretation. I also spent the subsequent six years writing a doctrinal PhD thesis, until my supervisor resigned. But nothing is ever wasted. Ironically, after being told by a teacher that I had gone as far as I was able, academically, I spent the next ten years as a teacher myself. I am convinced God has a real sense of humour.

5
God's Call

At the same time that my work with homeless men was drawing to an end and my teaching career was beginning, towards the end of 2008, I became part of a Christian motorcycle club called God's Squad.[6] In 2019, I also agreed to serve as European president within the club. Becoming a member of God's Squad was a clear calling from God, and one which has enabled me to draw on many of my previous experiences.

Many of the bikers with whom I come into contact have extremely sharp minds, are extremely down to earth and have an ability to see through pretences and insincerities. The biking subculture also sits very much on the fringes of society, holding distinctive values of authenticity and true brotherhood. Here, respect and loyalty remain important and, in a real sense, being part of a motorcycle club becomes an identity, something that permeates a person's very nature. These relationships can never be taken for granted, either, and some of these friendships have been among my most valued.

Within my own club, which celebrated its fiftieth anniversary in 2021, our call is primarily to the back patch world. Back patch-wearing bikers are identified by their own club colours, which they wear on the back of their leather or denim waistcoats, commonly identified as cut-offs. These colours, or back patches, contain imagery that identifies each particular club, along with the club's name and the area or country to

---

[6] www.gscmc.com (accessed 4th October 2023).

which they belong. Our own club colours contain a bright red cross, clearly identifying us as Christians, the name God's Squad, as well as each member's particular country or region. Wearing the club's colours is a heavy responsibility, and they are earned during what could be described as a period of apprenticeship and service. This is why membership in God's Squad takes a minimum of three years to attain, and then only with a clear calling and discernment.

Some of the rides I will recount have been with some of my own club brothers, as my role in the ministry often carries me across Europe and beyond. This is also why my own Harley is so important to me, as riding, maintaining and adapting it brings real attachment. This is even more significant, as the bike itself was in a real sense a gift from God, and while I have considered buying a new bike on many occasions, this is the one I believe God led me to, and the one I have been able to rely on during all my travels, just as God has never let me down as I have been riding it.

The final chapter in this journey through faith began in 2015, when I recognised the equally significant call to ministry in the Church of England. This still surprises me, not least owing to my determination not to conform to middle-class stereotypes or to deny my identity within the biking subculture.[7]

It was crucial that if God was calling me, He was calling me within my own identity, along with my existing ministries and giftings. It was also clear that this calling was not ultimately to any leafy suburb or affluent parish, but among those who resonated with my own experiences, which is why it was important not to allow myself to be transformed into a typical middle-class cleric. God has had His hand on this, and in the summer of 2022 I became vicar of St Peter's Church, Braunstone Park in Leicester, where I feel very much at home.

---

[7] www.bbc.co.uk/news/av/uk-england-leicestershire-45425842 (accessed 15th October 2023).

God doesn't call us to be someone else; He desires to use our personality, our experiences, our cultural identity. He may want to refine these, to enhance them, to add to them, but He calls us to be who He created us to be, with the experiences He leads us through. There is a clear journey that has led me to this point, not dissimilar to some of the rides I have taken, which I am about to describe, with the twists and turns, joys and disappointments, but always knowing that God is faithful on this long, exciting road of life and faith.

Part Two
The Road to Italy

6
Lessons on the Journey

It was the beginning of August 2014 when Alison climbed onto the Harley behind me to begin a trip we had been planning for some time. The plan was to ride the Harley as far as Pompeii, with roughly a week in the middle where we would relax in Rimini. We would also experience the fascinatingly varied cultures with which we would come into contact on the way, travelling two-up through nine European countries and principalities.

OK, the Harley in question did have an unusually high mileage, with 80,000 miles on the clock at that point, a noticeable gearbox leak and a set of indicators with a mind of their own, but what could possibly go wrong? A question I put to my wife as she frowned back at me, unconvinced, through the side mirror. It is true that we lost an indicator in France, along with a good quantity of oil, but that is par for the course.

Before we set off for the journey, we realised that we needed a set of saddlebags to fit everything in. Fortunately, I managed to source two original 1970s Harley Davidson leather panniers, located at the Isle of Dogs. We were not leaving until the following morning, and in my slightly deluded mind, this would give me plenty of time to ride over the day before, pick up the saddlebags, drill and form some new makeshift brackets, fit them to the bike, fix my indicators and finish packing. This in part explains why, a few days later, one of the rear indicators, which I had firmly attached using a cable tie, managed to dislodge, preferring to remain on the open roads of France.

The Isle of Dogs was 130 miles from our house, but before I had ridden halfway, the gear shifter rod broke. I managed to roll the bike down a slope and start it in fourth gear, then ride the sixty or so miles without stopping at roundabouts or traffic lights. The reality dawned, however, that without a shifter rod there was no way we could travel to Italy. It appeared that the trip was over before it had begun, as I knew I would need to order the part in.

I arrived at the house where the panniers were waiting, and asked if the owner had a cable tie to hold the broken rod in place, just to get me home. He disappeared into the garage and emerged with a brand-new shifter rod, which was the right length for the bike. He then offered to fit the rod for me, which he did. I asked him how much he wanted for it, but he refused to accept any money.

The fact was that if I hadn't ridden across to pick those panniers up, the trip would have been over in any case, as the shifter would have broken on the way to the ferry. The chances of a stranger, the day before the trip, having a brand-new linkage, the exact size we needed, sitting in his garage, was unimaginable, but nonetheless this was the case. I firmly believe that God had His hand on this one.

Once he had fitted the linkage, he appeared with the set of panniers, slightly embarrassed at their condition, although any problems were only cosmetic. Furthermore, he wouldn't accept more than £50 for them both, because of their condition, but in reality they have been an amazing set of panniers, and I would take them over any modern set produced today. In fact, they have been invaluable not only for that trip, but for the many others I have taken on this bike.

I sometimes wonder if some of us feel like we have been written off because of our external appearance, just like these panniers. But God looks within and sees our hearts, recognises our potential and is able to restore us, just like these saddlebags.

The panniers had a cheap veneer, which was attempting, and failing, to make them look new. The reality was that once I removed this veneer, the leather underneath was perfect. I could then apply some fresh leather dye to the faded and weather-worn exterior, before finally waterproofing them. While the panniers look a bit shabby now, after another 80,000 miles on the road, they are authentic, they are real and they are not trying to hide behind a cheap coating. They did need to lose the tassels, though, which were a little too authentic, looking great in the seventies but looking even better in the bottom of a drawer where they now reside.

Having fitted the panniers, loaded the bike and half-fixed the initial set of indicators, we were on our way. However, we were soon presented with one of the worst combinations of weather that seasoned bikers will at some point face – torrential rain and hurricane winds. With Alison on the back, this meant that the journey was far slower than it might have been if I had been riding solo. Furthermore, we experienced the added frustration of the predictable British motorway closures, and the inevitable detours with occasional signs presenting cryptic clues which might possibly lead in the right direction.

Having encountered countless traffic jams, filtered past tightly positioned lorries and squeezed through the infinitely narrowing gaps created by the steel-clad corridors of motionless vehicles, we emerged on the road to Dover and entered the usual race towards the ferry. We were now an hour and a half late, having missed our original sailing. We were cold, wet and barely made the last ferry of the day, which thankfully they allowed us to board.

After one of the worst rides to catch a ferry that I have ever experienced, we enjoyed a peaceful crossing, relaxing at a table, sampling a great British delicacy, consisting of coffee and malt loaf, while overlooking the vastness of the ever-changing aquatic landscape. We disembarked at Calais and made good progress, lodging for the night at St Quentin. We booked into a ground-floor room of a cheap motel. These lodgings are thankfully common in France, having little luxury, but ideal for travelling, and great for keeping an eye on the bike at night.

After passing our bags through the adjacent window into our room, we headed for a place to eat. We crossed a now redundant railway line and climbed on board an equally redundant dining carriage, which had once been filled with first-class passengers embarking on adventures through the open countryside of France. This transformed carriage had now ironically been converted into a working-class diner, serving cheap French wine and unusually lean steak. I was so hungry by this time that I could have eaten a horse, which I later found out was exactly what I had been eating.

After a relatively peaceful night, we were up with the dawn. I gave the bike a quick check over, only to find one of the rear indicators had become dislodged, possibly in the storm, and was swinging in the wind on its copper wire, like an out-of-control, iridescent chrome pendulum. Furthermore, its co-conspirator had decided to emancipate itself from the confines of the bike, preferring instead to find freedom from its enforced labour on the highways of France. As though this wasn't bad enough, on removing the dipstick I found the majority of the usually oil-encased gauge was as dry as a bone. It was now a matter of urgency for us to find a solution for these two issues. Failure to rectify the problems would result in being pulled over by the gendarme; I had previous unpleasant experiences of this, and always with unsatisfactory outcomes. Even more serious, though, was the lack of engine oil, which could quickly result in the engine seizing up and would herald the swift demise of the bike.

In the case of the indicators, these perpetually deteriorating lights had gradually been becoming increasingly disengaged from their very life source. As each seemingly insignificant strand of wire broke away, the intensity of light dimmed almost imperceptibly, to the extent to which their life was eventually extinguished, with one preferring now the darkness of a cold, lonely road.

This disconnect can be equally experienced within our walk with God, as we gradually become disengaged from the source, failing to notice the imperceptible but steady decay of a once-empowering relationship. With each strand of wire losing the capacity to draw the life-giving current which had allowed those indicators to be truly effective, their purpose was fading; they had become merely ineffectual, decorative chrome shells. It is possible, too, for us to lose our purpose, becoming so disconnected with God that we lose our effectiveness, merely going through the motions, indistinguishable from those now decorative shells that were devoid of light.

It was true, there was a point of no return for one of the indicators, as it severed itself from the bike, preferring the darkness of the empty road, but not necessarily for the remaining indicator. I might have recognised this disconnection if I had paid more attention and re-established its relationship to the source. Even with one strand there would have been hope, and some of us are holding on with one strand, and there is hope.

For a light once hidden, once visually imperceptible, as if it had been placed under a bowl, there is the possibility of renewal. God can once more recreate the emanating brightness of a blazing torch, as we place our light high upon a lampstand, as Jesus suggests in Luke 8:16. If we regain our connection, we will withstand the storms of life, and our lights will continue to shine brightly, because they will reflect Christ's light.

Having jettisoned one indicator and with its twin needing intensive care, we began our search for a bike shop within St Quentin, and managed to purchase some replacement indicators. We also eventually located a tool outlet where we acquired connectors, tape and a circuit-testing screwdriver in order to fit these flashing beacons to the vehicle. This time the twin indicators clung as tightly as a pair of chrome-coated limpet shells, holding fast to their steel-encrusted rock, impervious to the tidal onslaughts, which they would be facing when we later found ourselves caught in the middle of a full-blown flood!

More importantly, the internal life of the bike was still critically at risk of collapsing, in its desperate need for engine oil. This precious lifeblood at the heart of the bike was as imperative for the bike ride as the fluid that keeps our joints from seizing is imperative to our movements, and to fail to sort this out rapidly would end in equal disaster. This particular life blood at the time was the makers' recommended mineral oil for the bike. I have since started using an alternative established brand of semi-synthetic, which seems to suit it better, but here it was important to top up with the same type that was already in the engine. We fortunately discovered that there was a dealership in Reims, and so we anxiously headed off, hoping the engine would not seize up before we arrived.

With no internet connection, we found ourselves riding aimlessly along the antiquated streets of Reims, searching for the Harley dealership, which was like searching for a needle in a haystack. There were few people on the streets, and none was able to converse in a language we could understand. As always, we were praying for some divine direction as we pulled up next to an aged lady. Predictably, again we lacked the verbal skills to ask for help. However, this didn't mean she was unable to communicate, as she broke into an animated performance, mimicking one of those overenthusiastic traffic officers, waving in all directions as they summon drivers forward. She disappeared into a neighbour's house and returned with a friendly, bilingual Frenchman. Furthermore, he not only offered to give us directions to the shop, but he also climbed into his car and beckoned us to follow. We tailed the car for fifteen minutes, through the twists and turns within the backstreets of Reims, and he led us finally into the car park of a Harley dealer.

This selfless help made me realise how much influence we can have by one generous act. He put himself out for no reward, making me appreciate the kindness of strangers. In fact, the writer of Hebrews tells us that this hospitality to strangers is important, and that 'some people have shown hospitality to angels without knowing it' (Hebrews 13:2). As he drove off after we thanked him, we approached the door of the shop that would hold the key to this precious life-giving elixir. As we pushed the door, we noticed the sign, which almost mockingly indicated that it was closed all day! There was nothing for it; we were forced to spend the night in a fairly grotty motel. However, despite the enforced stay, we enjoyed a traditional French breakfast, which included croissants that far exceeded the expectations gained from the inadequate copies found in England. To our relief, the Harley shop was open in the morning, and we were able to restore the balance of the engine's oil.

My faulty indicators were obvious, but when it comes to oil, this is an internal issue, and without sufficient oil the whole journey comes to an abrupt halt. This is true again of our spiritual journeys, and it is striking here that the Holy Spirit has always been symbolised with oil – just as the bike is filled with oil, unnoticed but permeating the whole engine, unseen but affecting each part and being evident in its performance, so too we are encouraged to be filled with the Holy Spirit, an unseen helper, comforter and guide who sustains our internal spiritual life, freeing, empowering and protecting us.[8] Moreover, while being unseen, He remains evident through the way we lead our lives, through the way we walk, through the way we love others. I will never know if our guide who put himself out for us had faith, but I was hopeful that God was at work in his life.

On leaving Reims, we headed towards Basel in Switzerland, and after a fairly easy initial journey, the satnav completely died. We again had no idea where we were or what direction to take. We had also taken a scenic route, which meant that there were no firm landmarks. We finally asked another Frenchman, a lorry driver this time, for directions, and he proceeded to direct us through a series of back roads which wound through all manner of terrain. The journey took us ten hours, along sharp winding lanes as we passed unfamiliar towns and negotiated narrow

---

[8] John 14:15-17; Acts 1:4-8.

tracks. We finally reached Mulhouse, having been sent on a wild goose chase, and which was completely out of our way.

This almost threatened to undermine all the goodwill we had received from our previously positive experience in Reims. From Mulhouse we travelled forty kilometres, crossing the border to Basel. Unfortunately, the realisation dawned that even the cheapest hotel in Basel was beyond our means. Not only that, but Basel seemed to have an air of superiority, and so we rode back across the border, returning more than an hour later to where we had first begun in Mulhouse. Fortunately, the border guards were too busy to notice the same bike nipping into their country before immediately nipping back out, which would have been sure to raise unwanted attention.

In Mulhouse we discovered extremely friendly people, cheap but satisfactory food and an air of authenticity, unlike Basel. We spent a relaxing night before rising for breakfast and once more heading to Basel, where we again crossed the same border for the third time in twenty-four hours, and were finally heading for the Swiss Alps.

7

Detours and Perspectives

The initial route to the Alps appeared fairly unimaginative, travelling along straight, mundane roads with little character. However, in drawing ever closer, a gradual transformation began, as we passed through the increasingly dramatic scenery and rode past undulating fields containing the sudden movements of four-legged beasts retreating into the safety of the hillside woods. These wonderful natural surroundings began to uncover collections of picturesque Swiss cabins, set perfectly within this wonderful scenery, the type one may find on a typical picture postcard or a classic biscuit tin. These wooden cabins fit unobtrusively within their idyllic landscapes, scattered along the hillside like hay bales in a farmer's field.

The truly breathtaking moment, though, occurred when the vastness of the Alps suddenly emerged, seemingly from nowhere. I would defy anyone to fail to be overwhelmed, seeing this view for the first time, as these great rock sentinels stand defiantly, refusing to be ignored, or passed without recognition. This left us with a decision to make: how to negotiate these great stone monoliths. As we drew ever nearer, we needed to decide whether to negotiate the alpine pass across the top of the mountain or to take the long, laborious miles of tunnels leading into Italy. In view of time restraints, we initially decided to take the tunnels, which led directly through the heart of the mountains. After twenty tedious minutes, I decided I couldn't stand it. We were here to enjoy the journey, and a set of long, straight tunnels was not my idea of fun. I decided to negotiate a somewhat risky U-turn across the four lanes within the tunnel, to a cacophony of car horns. We then rode back along the twenty-minute journey through the tunnel, leading to where we had first entered, and onto the mountain pass.

There was a real sense of freedom as we left the traffic behind and climbed steadily along the steep, single-track inclines, the smell of burning clutch oil accompanying the noise of the straining engine. Onwards and upwards, though, through the dense alpine clouds, finally emerging into a transformed world filled with an iridescent and dazzling sunlight. The air was clean and fresh as we wound steadily across the mountain pass. We were passed only by the odd biker who would shake their leg, which appeared to be a friendly greeting, as they flew by. Lunchtime approached, so we made the most of the breathtaking views, sitting at a deserted bench overlooking an incredible mountain range, with not a person in sight.

After an incredible ride across the Alps, we finally found ourselves descending into what seemed extremely familiar territory. What we hadn't realised was that we had inadvertently missed a turn, which would have brought us out on the other side, but instead we ended up riding in a long circle, leading us back to where we started!

The decision was unilaterally made from the rear of the bike to take the safe option, back beneath the mountains we had just crossed. We subsequently took the long, straight route for a second time, along the miles of barely lit tunnels. The rows of lights, glowing from the apex of the tunnel, led into the endless emptiness ahead, while at the same time becoming almost hypnotic.

We continued along this luminescent grotto, carved into the heart of the mountain, until it emerged once more into the dazzling sunlight, revealing a beautiful blue sky. Although we had lost time initially doubling back in order to cross those mountain peaks, it proved to be one of the highlights of the trip. It isn't possible to recreate those breathtaking views, or even to adequately describe how amazing it is to be in such an inspiring place.

There are times when we need to hold on to those mountaintop experiences, those memories that sustain us. To hold on when our journey leads us into the darkness and despair of those seemingly ceaseless tunnels. However, in those dark times, we can hold on to the knowledge and hope that they will indeed end, that we don't have to travel them alone, and that they will lead once more into the light.

For the great psalmist, David, as well as the mountaintop experiences with God, he experienced the darkness of those unending tunnels. Even in this, he was able to express his confidence in God's protection within the poetic phrases of a psalm where he writes, 'Even though I walk through the darkest valley, I will fear no evil, for you are with me' (Psalm 23:4). Those mountaintop experiences are so important, even when they are unintended or emerging from a wrong turn. There are times when we feel slightly lost in life too. However, sometimes we need to make the most of the moment, to find some blessing in our detours. We may find blessings in our wanderings too.

Once across the Alps, we headed for Blevio and Lake Como. As we approached the lake, we were reminded once more that the satnav was dead, and the evening was drawing in rapidly. We weaved through narrow lanes, passing silhouettes of long wooden sailing masts, standing proud and still in the moonlight. We could hear the gentle lapping of the water, caressing the shale that lay beneath, lapping against the raised wooden jetties. There were glimpses of moonlit waves being gently coaxed by the evening breeze as they danced across this large expanse of water which made up Lake Como. We peered above the drystone wall as we moved along the water line, following our trajectory through villages bereft of life, finally losing hope of ever finding our lodgings, having weaved aimlessly among these barely lit, deserted Italian villages for hours.

We eventually came upon a solitary pizza establishment, although the place was now closed. As we pulled up, we found an Italian man sitting outside. We didn't really know how far away we were from our desired destination; it could have been ten minutes or ten miles. It was now gone 11.30 at night, and this felt like our last chance, as this was the first person we had seen for hours; in fact, this was the first stop we had made since crossing the Italian border. With little hope that this stranger would even have heard of the place we were trying to find, we had rehearsed the negative answer in our heads.

The reply, however, was totally unexpected. Not only did he know where this place was, but he could almost point to it. He commenced by describing what would have been a short walk up a steep winding lane, which gently arched towards our lodgings.

We climbed on the bike once more and headed up this short lane, pulling up outside a set of steep stone steps, almost hidden by the darkness. Unsurprisingly, the owner wasn't impressed by our late arrival, and so after putting the bike in his garage, we made a swift retreat to our room, which revealed an extremely disappointing view. While we were relieved to have found our lodgings, we were having second thoughts about staying here for a couple of nights.

We awoke the next morning, however, as the sun shone brightly through our window, transforming the dismal view from the night before into the most stunning backdrop. Now, in the clear light of day, we were able to gaze down onto this beautiful lakeside view which had been hidden by the darkness as we first arrived. We stepped out of our room and emerged onto an incredible veranda, which also overlooked the expanse of the lake. It had actually been worth the hours of riding to search for this wonderful home, as we enjoyed an Italian coffee with our breakfast on this makeshift veranda, surrounded by vines and overlooking the spectacular lakeside views, which were now bathed in sunlight, revealing the surrounding traditional Italian harbour towns. We had, in fact, ridden through some of these towns on the way up to our lodgings;

however, from our vantage point, the whole lake was transformed.

We spent the day riding around the lake, stopping off at various points of interest, enjoying the views of this now utterly transformed lake. We made the mistake of ordering pizza with a cold beer at one point, from a lakeside café; it was obviously designed for tourists and didn't have a clue how to make pizza.

In the evening, we once more sat out overlooking the spectacular views from the veranda, with the moon now reflecting off the water, as we were joined by another couple.

As we ate, and sampled some great Italian wine, we spent the evening enjoying a fascinating conversation with fellow travellers from Holland, who had come down from the further reaches of Italy. Here, we also discovered some interesting and invaluable facts, such as the lake was in the shape of an epsilon! Well, this snippet of information was so intriguing to my wife, being the most memorable thing she took away from the conversation. This mysterious epsilon-shaped lake sounded extremely exotic to Alison, who imagined all sorts of intricate permutations surrounding this water.

However, the cold reality of this mysterious epsilon lost its mystique weeks later, when I explained that this was actually just a big Greek letter Y. Discovering that the lake was Y-shaped didn't have the same ring to it. It's a bit like trying to sell the wonderfully bourgeois *escargot*, which is so popular within the many exclusive restaurants around France, and finding out the cold, hard truth that it is merely a garlic-coated garden snail.

Having spent an amazing evening overlooking the lake, we decided to spend some more time the following day riding around this great expanse of Y-shaped water, through the familiar sunlit harbour towns and villages, which again had been transformed by the daylight.

It is interesting how much of a difference reviewing our perspective can make to a situation. We had now seen this lake and its surrounding villages from three different vantage points. All three revealed the same physical structures, the same villages, the same roads, all three with completely different perspectives.

Sometimes we need to change our vantage point, to see things differently, to step into the light in order for our clouded vision to be transformed. We need to move our eyes upwards, where we can see the bigger picture. We were certainly praying as we rode through those darkened streets, and as we found this haven on the hillside our perspective was immediately transformed.

This change of perspective was also captured within the New Testament narrative of a man who had been born without sight.[9] As Jesus did something out of the ordinary, in spitting into the man's eyes before touching them, the man's perspective was immediately changed. Light had entered his vision, but he could see only people appearing to look like trees. However, when Jesus touched his eyes for a second time, his perspective was corrected as the intensity of light streamed into his vision. He was able to see life as it really was. Jesus allowed him to see the big picture, to see clearly, bringing light to bear on a once darkened world.

Those Italian villages lit up by the sun were amazing, looking out onto the water from the narrow streets. Though they were nothing compared to the views from the hillside on that makeshift veranda, which enabled us to see the big picture, the immensity of this awe-inspiring lake.

---

[9] Mark 8:22-26.

8
Culture, Scars and Different Wine

Having spent two relaxing days at Lake Como, we were back on the road and heading for Verona. Time to get some culture! Having been unable to find an affordable hotel in Verona, we checked into a cheap place on the outskirts of the town. We then climbed back onto the bike and headed for this small Italian cultural centre. We pulled up next to a group of pristine Honda Gold Wing motorcycles, along with their equally pristine riders. We could feel the tangible animosity in the air as soon as we arrived. They obviously resented the fact that this row of beautifully gleaming, plastic-encased vehicles was being ruined by an ageing Harley Davidson.

We climbed off the road-beaten bike, along with its beautiful bronze patina, which we had collected from the miles spent on the road. The passenger on the Gold Wing that was parked next to us was clothed in immaculate but impractical Italian fashion leathers. The passenger climbed down in tandem with Alison, who was wearing a jacket which had seen plenty of life. There was an obvious look of contempt from the Gold Wing owner as the two ladies stood looking at each other, not dissimilar to the looks I received as I climbed down in my more extreme weather-beaten jacket. The scene reminded me of a bike trip in America, where we passed a couple of peacocks that appeared to be desperate to show us how wonderfully decadent they were as they compensated for their slight stature with enormous multicoloured fan-like tails. It appeared that we had stumbled across the peacocks of the biking world.

This display reminded me of the tragic Greek myth of Echo and Narcissus, where Echo could only repeat back what was spoken to her, so that when she fell in love with Narcissus, she couldn't adequately express it. Her advances were rejected in any case, as Narcissus caught sight of his own reflection in the river. Narcissus then fell in love with his own reflection, being all-consumed before eventually being metamorphosed into a flower in the forest.

As we climbed off the bikes, any attempt we made at a greeting was unreciprocated, which was not unexpected and was actually fine. Sadly, their somewhat narcissistic traits, revealed in their outward appearance and their apparent need for those around to affirm the worth of their motorcycles, seemed more important than making foreign travellers feel welcome. This experience stands as a reminder to remain welcoming, whatever someone's outward appearance.

This need for validation is nothing new. The religious leaders within the New Testament required this same validation, needing to look good in front of the crowds. On the contrary, Jesus suggested, our good deeds need to be done in secret. This is where we gain our validation, from God, who sees all that we do.[10] In doing this, we keep our inner integrity intact, not needing to seek validation from others.

This teaching from Jesus certainly resonated as we pulled up next to these bikes in Verona, and I would certainly have taken my road-beaten Harley over any of these immaculate, showroom, polished motorcycles!

Stepping onto the pavement, we walked past the row of bikes. We found that the town was full of character, revealing some fascinating ancient Italian architecture. The narrow side streets were lined with traditional stores, drawing in the window shoppers and tourists alike. There was a feeling of culture, of

---

[10] Matthew 6:1-4.

nostalgia, of an ancient history, seeping from the very foundations of each and every building. There was a tangible atmosphere that radiated from the occupants of this culturally distinct town. A sort of combined identity exuded to create this sense that we were walking on ancient ground. Verona, as with any Italian town, is renowned for its coffee, and this particular town was scattered with small bistros, where it was possible to drink coffee while standing at a classic table, which we did, having ordered two espressos.

After this exquisite Italian coffee, which only the Italians can create, we approached the centre square. We were presented with an ancient and imposing stone amphitheatre, towering high above all of these ancient buildings. We noticed that *Madame Butterfly* was being presented in this overpowering structure in three-quarters of an hour's time, which I suggested would be an enriching cultural experience.

The original intention was to go out for a meal, having not eaten for hours. While not completely on board with the idea, Alison eventually agreed to grab a sausage roll and buy two of the cheapest tickets for the show, which were furthest away from the stage, and get ready to be immersed in the experience.

The opera tells the story of Madame Butterfly, a young Japanese *geisha*, who falls in love with an American US Navy lieutenant and agrees to marry him. However, he is really stringing her along, and ultimately wants an American wife. He leaves for America, marries another woman and returns years later, to find he has a son. Having waited for the lieutenant, who now wants to take his son back to America, and having lost everything by becoming an outcast when she converted to Christianity, she finally takes her own life. Quite a tragic plot, but despite the sadness of the story, it would prove to be a real joy to be part of this rich Italian atmosphere.

We left our helmets in the cloakroom and made our way up the ancient stone steps to the very top of the open-air theatre. In reality, these turned out to be the best seats we could have booked. We were entertained by an over-exuberant Italian man, who constantly stood up and cheered in all the wrong places, being told off by an equally exuberant Italian wife. From there we could not only see the vastness of the amphitheatre, but we were also able to experience the authentic Italian atmosphere, sitting among real people. On top of that, we were treated to a stunning performance of *Madame Butterfly*, which it would be impossible to recreate anywhere else in the world. At one point I jokingly said, 'It's just a shame we are listening to it in Italy, as we can't understand what they are singing about!' My wife agreed for a while, until the penny eventually dropped that the opera is written and therefore performed in Italian.

Culture now over, we had decided to spend a week in Rimini, to break up the three weeks of riding. The room had appeared cheap, but in reality was relatively expensive for what it was – a glorified walk-in cupboard with a bed. The room had the luxury of a shower, but with some unique design features, including a bidet in the corner of the shower unit itself. Despite this, it had been a good idea to spend the week there, as it gave us a chance to relax, stroll down the beach and enjoy a glass of excellent wine or the odd bottle of Italian beer.

We were able to visit the famous San Marino while there, which appeared in the form of a magnificent ancient town, built on a mountainside. It contained steep, winding lanes, a fairy-tale castle, and shops selling a combination of jewellery, soft toys and weaponry, including swords, crossbows and knives. A strange combination, you may think! You could literally go in for a stuffed bear and come out with the implements to stuff a bear with. San Marino was actually a sovereign state, one of the remnants of several principalities which could once be found in Italy. This made sense of its awe-inspiring castle, built on that imposing mountainside. Standing on top of San Marino, we were able to look down on the town below, watching vehicles driving around the base of the mountain, looking like model cars racing around a track. The vantage point was perfectly situated to defend this small principality, with the ability to look down on all potential invaders who may have been unwise enough to attempt to scale the sheer climb. Now, its only invaders consisted of foreign tourists armed with cameras and guidebooks.

As we made our way back down the steep, winding paths, we once more passed the weaponry and soft toy store. After much deliberation, I decided against purchasing a broadsword as a present for Alison. I figured that it may have been a little overkill for chopping onions, as well as the fact that a six-foot sword probably wouldn't quite fit in the panniers. My mind also returned to the memory of disappointment on Alison's face as I presented her with a wok and a meat cleaver one Valentine's Day, realising that she had been tempted to try the cleaver out there and then, and I certainly didn't want to risk the potential injury that a broadsword could do. So we returned to the bike and headed back to Rimini after a fascinating day in San Marino.

The week had gone smoothly and without any dramas, until we decided to find a beach a couple of days before we needed to leave, so Alison could go for a swim. However, she insisted on not needing to wear long trousers on the journey back. No amount of reasoning would dissuade her, with the final words, 'I'm an adult, I won't touch the exhaust, and I take full responsibility if I get burned.' The problem is that in extreme heat, the exhaust can reach temperatures akin to a domestic griddle, enabling it to cook a steak in seconds, which is exactly what Alison's calf looked like as she climbed off the bike in immense pain. We spent the next half-hour riding round searching for a store that stocked frozen food. We located a small supermarket, headed for the frozen goods area and, with the stealth of a couple of ninjas, applied several packs of frozen peas onto Alison's leg, avoiding being spotted by the owner. I was surprised that the dazzling heat emanating from her leg didn't alert the owner to this covert operation, or even set off the fire alarms, but thankfully the pain was eventually eased enough to carry on. There is a lesson here, as she still carries the remnants of those pretty severe burns.

The Christian journey is a bit like this at times. All may be going well, as God helps us to navigate the route, allowing us to enjoy the journey. Then things so often begin to get a little hot, a little difficult, and the things we know we should do appear to us to be restricting our freedom. Usually these are the things which, at first sight, appear appealing, but more often than not we find that what appeared to be restricting our freedom was actually safeguarding it, bringing us security. Sometimes we recognise this, and allow God to bring healing. However, at times there are scars, and we can carry those scars for a long time, just as my wife does on her leg, even though they are greatly faded now. Needless to say, she hasn't insisted on wearing shorts on the bike again.

Having had a relaxing week in Rimini, we decided to spend our last day wandering along the seafront. We ambled past the endless array of identical beach umbrellas, suspended above the sand like enormous multicoloured parachutes, lined up seemingly with military precision. Beneath these oversized parasols lay semiconscious Italian bodies, laid out, legs akimbo, on their sterile plastic stretchers. Some of the more careless among them glowed with a bright red hue, suggesting that some of these sunbeds might actually have been better placed in an A&E department.

We walked past two infamous sun loungers, which we had naively claimed when we first arrived in Rimini, not realising the Italians booked them exclusively for the week on these private beaches and would be prepared to defend them with their lives. We had discovered this as we lay on tandem loungers, enjoying the views, as the blazing sun radiated across a clear blue Italian sky. Suddenly we had been presented with an Italian man, acting as if his home was being burgled and he had just come across the culprits in the act. I had surmised that he had taken part in an English course at some point in his life, which began and ended with the single but apparently essential phrase of 'go away'.

At first we were bemused, but soon came to the realisation that maybe these loungers were not actually freely available to the general public. After several failed attempts using my de-escalation skills and subtle mediation techniques, we worried that he might actually have a coronary there and then, or even do himself some serious physical harm. We had therefore left the scene and returned to the promenade.

We walked a little further and came, purely by chance, upon a local wine-tasting event. Here, we wandered past several makeshift stalls festooned along the seafront, with copious bottles of wine from various regions set out on the large wooden tables, like skittles ready to be demolished. This was certainly an eye-opener, as we entered into the spirit of the occasion. We were given a wafer-thin wine glass, which we later carried, undamaged, across Europe. We were then handed a wine-glass-carrying pouch, which made us look like a couple of alcoholic kangaroos. These were a great idea, though, as they allowed us to wander the stalls, carrying our wine, with both hands free. Finally, we were presented with several tickets, which could be exchanged for several glasses of wine.

We discovered quickly that all wine is not equal. We opted first for an expensive red Italian wine, which I imagine was rich in body, with hints of blackberry, but I could be wrong. We were surprised at the meagre quantity we received; however, this really was a tasting experience, and the wine itself was exquisite. We next moved to a stall with a much cheaper Albanian wine. I was curious to see what Albanian wine tasted like in comparison. Initially, things were looking up as the owner poured almost a full glass. However, I then understood the actual rules of the game. The quantity of wine we received really was determined by its quality, and this particular glass could have stripped four coats of paint from an old door.

Thinking about the large quantity of this particular Albanian wine reminded me of the generosity of Jesus, as He turned water into wine at a local wedding. Jesus recognised the embarrassment that running out of wine would cause to the wedding couple and responded with compassion. However, for Jesus, the quality of the wine didn't depend on its quantity, unlike our own wine-tasting experience. Jesus provided a generous amount of wine, but He also provided the very best.[11] Jesus is often able to surprise us with His generosity and compassion, as with this wine. For both myself and Alison, it was a wonderful final day, sipping wine next to the beach as the sun set on a perfect horizon.

After a relaxing week in Rimini, we were now eager to continue our journey. So the next day, we saddled up, pulling on our protective gear and setting off for what was to prove a life-threatening journey to Rome.

---

[11] John 2:1-11

9
Storms and Treasures

As we left Rimini the weather changed, and we experienced a strange sensation on our faces. Yes, it was actually starting to rain, but we hadn't reckoned on the extent or intensity that was yet to come. We had decided to take the scenic route to Rome and so started to wind our way through narrow streets, passing through ominously deserted villages. As we rode across the cobbled, uneven roads, the rain turned into a full-blown storm. The as-of-yet watertight jackets soaked up the torrent of water, which was being thrown at us in bucketloads, and every stitch of clothing was now saturated. I was wearing a heated waistcoat, which I immediately regretted, as the wiring began to short circuit, producing electric shocks under my jacket. The rain became torrential, and the water reached the base of the engine as the lanes turned into rivers.

I hadn't a clue what I was riding over as the cobbled street was completely submerged. We realised we were caught in a full-blown flood. From the back seat, Alison was very animated and insistent that we needed to stop, adding the odd comment like, 'We are going to die!' Stopping wasn't an option, however, partly owing to the ever-rising waters and the fact that we were now in serious danger of hypothermia. So we rode through the rivers with the real possibility that the engine would be swamped. We weaved our way past abandoned cars, looking more like boats moored at the side of a river than four-wheeled means of transportation.

We eventually reached the highway and made our way along the central barrier where the water was slightly shallower. As we rode steadily upwards, the water began to subside, and although unable to feel fingers or toes, we were thankfully still breathing.

We finally approached Rome, and found our hotel without much trouble, which fortunately we had pre-booked on this occasion and which happened to be the classiest place we had yet stayed in. We entered the lobby, where other guests in semi-formal wear were heading for afternoon tea. We looked like a couple of drowned rats as we squelched across the floor to check in. We couldn't have created a bigger pool of water if we had just stepped out of a swimming pool. We were given our keys and pointed to an elevator, which was worrying, as we may well have shorted the electrics as the water continued to pour steadily from our clothing. However, after finding the room, and following several attempts to fit the key in the door as our hands shook violently with little feeling in our fingers, we entered the warmth. Here, we spent a good half-hour under a warm shower, waiting for the feeling to return to our extremities.

This experience, again, is reminiscent of those journeys through life in which we sometimes find ourselves, riding the storm, caught in situations which we feel are out of our control. Often when we are moving through these deep waters, it can seem like there is no way through, as we struggle to keep afloat. Sometimes we may feel that we just want to stop, to give up, losing hope that there is a way through. We felt a little like those disciples on the Sea of Galilee, caught in the storm, being swamped with water as Jesus slept. But those disciples, filled with anxiety, struggling to see the shore were not alone. Jesus was in the boat, and eventually brought calm to the storm.[12]

This sense that Jesus was in this storm with us, protecting, reassuring, acting, was my own experience in that flood. It wasn't a pain-free experience, as hypothermia loomed extremely

---

[12] Mark 4:35-41.

close, along with the pain of severe numbness in the fingertips which all bikers will have some experience of. I knew that God was with us as we negotiated those waters, calming any anxiety, bringing us once more to firm ground. I firmly believe that we are not alone through those storms of life, that we can turn to the One who is able to steer us through the waters, who can calm the fiercest of storms as we journey on through life together. Fortunately, the weather transformed into warm sunlit days for the remainder of the time, and we were able to enjoy some of this well-needed sun.

Having slept well, and recovered from the turbulent journey, we were able to explore Rome for a few days. We rode across to the immense and imposing Colosseum, which put Verona's amphitheatre in the shade. We climbed the steps to the pinnacle of this great structure, overlooking Rome from all directions and looking down onto an area where the sometimes-barbaric entertainment would have occurred. We sat for a moment on the ancient stone seats, where emperors and subjects would have sat for various games. We descended the steps back towards the base of this enormous yet claustrophobic structure, moving closer to its very bowels with its walls containing thick iron shackles, its trapdoors and the desolation of its stone enclosures. Here, there was a stark reminder of the gladiatorial games that took place there, where men fought for their lives before thousands of eager spectators.

The base of the Colosseum was reminiscent of circular zoological enclosures, designed to separate potentially ferocious animals from visitors, but on a mammoth scale. Ironically, this enormous enclosure also separated those early Christian martyrs, who refused to deny their faith, from the crowds looking down upon them. This undeniable architectural marvel held mixed feelings, standing as a testimony to a time of greatness, while the thick stone walls carried memories of despair. However, even in this despair there was also hope embedded within the rock. In refusing to deny the most precious thing that those early Christians possessed, a faith in

Christ, which couldn't be shaken, they were able, I believe, to continue their own journey to a place of eternal peace.

The following morning, we rose for an early start, as we were riding to our furthest destination of the trip. We were heading for Pompeii, along with its semi-dormant volcano. The ride was spectacular, following the coastal road with its stunning views, looking over the crystal blue Tyrrhenian Sea. Pompeii was four hours away via the coast road, which led through the city of Naples.

Pompeii was steeped in history, and a reminder of the great eruption of a volcano that decimated everything within its reach. The volcano erupted with such explosive power and pace that the whole of Pompeii was engulfed. Pompeii was a unique place, though, with the memory of life in this ancient Roman province, literally trapped in time. Walking along the excavated lanes, with ancient villas scattered around, along with the more dominating monuments and structures, was both enlightening and sobering. The plaster casts created from those ancient inhabitants, frozen in their final movements, appeared somewhat encased in despair. Some of these inhabitants were sleeping, others going about their normal everyday business, but none escaped.

Pompeii was certainly an interesting place, as it unfolded the secrets of this ancient civilisation. The most striking feature of Pompeii is the very source of its destruction – the semi-dormant volcano, Mount Vesuvius. Having this grumbling warning of potential destruction on your doorstep, we might imagine that it would put anyone off from living there, but this isn't the case, as whole communities live within range of its threatening destructive power.

We returned to the bike and left this vast memory of loss, heading now for the volcano itself. We decided to ride the steep incline along the side of the volcano, heading as far as we were permitted. We stopped not far from the summit, trying to imagine what it would have been like to have been there when this great mountain exploded into life, sending scalding fumes and molten lava towards the sea, via Pompeii. We picked up a tangible reminder of this place in the shape of a small piece of solidified lava, which would have once streamed from the bowels of the earth.

Standing there, looking out over this once living, breathing community, acknowledging those now motionless figures, one cannot fail to consider one's own mortality. Here, we wondered what their thoughts were at that final moment, as the ash engulfed their world, without time to prepare and without warning.

I was reminded of Jesus' own warning that no one knows the time or the hour of His return, and His subsequent advice to be ready, giving the analogy that, if the owner of the house knew when the thief was arriving, he would have been watching to prevent the break-in.[13]

Having reflected for a while, we returned to Rome by the more direct route. We took our lives into our hands as the unpredictable Italian motorists performed all manner of illegal manoeuvres, not least in joining us in the fast lane as we were overtaking a car, nearly scraping the handlebars as they sped past at well over 100 miles an hour. We enjoyed our night in Rome, though, and looked forward to the next day.

On our final morning in Rome, we climbed back on the bike for a trip to Vatican City. We entered a great square, where hundreds of adherents had gathered to hear a message from the Pope. The atmosphere was electric, reminiscent of the anticipation within a football stadium, then deafening chants, piercing air horns and jubilant cheers resounded. The Pope appeared at a window, silencing the crowd as he gave an address in Italian.

We then moved across a great open square, and entered the doors of the Vatican itself, the wealth on view being only a fraction of the treasures stored away. As we moved from room to room, it was also quite intriguing to consider what may be hidden within those walls.

---

[13] Matthew 24:42-44.

There were invaluable paintings created by the great masters, enormous marble carvings, as well as ancient Christian artefacts. Some of these were located in the famous Sistine Chapel. Within this chapel, we moved slowly with the masses, looking upwards at the fresco painted by Michelangelo, while finding a friendly hand on my shoulder from a security guard as I photographed these great works of art, ironically standing next to a sign instructing no photographs! It is difficult to describe how overwhelming these paintings were, demanding our attention from above. We stood looking upwards at one of his most famous paintings, depicting the finger of God, reaching out to Adam's almost disinterested outstretched hand. It was also quite humbling, gazing at this painting, interpreting in it the lengths God went to in order to reach out to us when we were equally disinterested.

We finally moved beyond the Sistine Chapel, back into the main building. Here, we were presented with a group of realistic statues, distributed along the walls of long corridors, and a room filled with silent stationary beings trapped in time. As we moved among these life-sized carvings of people, animals and mythical beasts, I was starkly reminded of the courtyard in Narnia, where the followers of Aslan had been turned to stone.[14] Moving within this ominous atmosphere was certainly a strange experience.

As I considered this enormous wealth hidden within these walls, and much of it hidden away in storerooms and cupboards, I reflected on the way Jesus lived and what He taught about wealth. The room full of cold stone-hearted figures could almost have been a structural parable explaining the consequences of storing up treasures on earth, rather than storing up treasure in heaven, as Jesus teaches in Matthew 6:19-21. Jesus had compassion for the poor, the oppressed and the outcasts, which is revealed in the various Gospels.

---

[14] C S Lewis, *The Lion, the Witch, and the Wardrobe* (London: HarperCollins, 2014).

The Vatican was an impressive place to visit, and a fascinating destination. However, there was also a feeling of walking into a mausoleum, particularly on entering this vault full of inanimate, lifeless, stone statues. In fact, I was happy to return to the sunlit streets, back among the living, ambling along with ordinary people on the streets of Rome.

We eventually arrived back at the bike and decided to do some touring around the local backstreets of Rome. While this was interesting, it was far from relaxing. This was a city that appeared to have no traffic laws. At first the lack of indicating and racing to overtake bikes and cars on the left or right appeared strange. But the longer you spend among the craziness, the more this type of riding seems normal. So much so that in one wide intersection, which was crammed with over-revving mopeds stretching far behind us, and at least five astride of us, we were treated to a kind of chaotic petrol-fuelled dance. As the lights changed, mopeds could be seen crisscrossing in front of each other, weaving both ways across four lanes of busy traffic, horns blazing, tyres screeching and metal grinding, as the bikes made contact with each other. Fortunately, we were at the front and were able to pull away fast enough to leave the carnage behind. It was certainly an eye-opening ride that day.

10

The Journey Unfolds

We had originally decided to visit Venice after Rome, but instead decided to take a detour in order to visit Florence. We headed for the hotel room, which we had booked at a reasonable rate, only to find that we were unable to gain access, with no sign of the owner. We also realised why it had been so reasonably priced in a city like Florence, as we noticed the bars on the windows, along with the fact that we were actually miles away from the main cultural centre. Feeling pretty fed up by now, and unable to get to our room, we decided to have a wander around what looked like a fairly rough neighbourhood. In fact, there was little to see, with just a couple of local sparsely stocked shops, and several dubious-looking youths.

We ambled back to the hotel, where the owner had now arrived. Inside was actually much better than its rough exterior had led us to believe. The owner was a friendly Italian man with a good grasp of English, and gave us a recommendation for a local restaurant. We changed out of our bike gear and headed down to this establishment. However, on arrival, we wondered if we were even in the right place, as we entered the door of a family home. To our relief, we found that they did actually prepare and serve food, and in their back yard they had arranged some rudimentary tables and a seating area. What was presented to us was both unexpected and somewhat astonishing. From the limited menu of pasta or pizza, we ordered the pizza. We were then presented with this truly amazing homemade meal, which was accompanied by a bottle of local wine, which was equally astonishing. In fact, sitting there in this traditional home, enjoying this authentic pizza and wine, in the perfect Italian temperature, proved to be one of the most amazing experiences of the trip.

This one meal in this idyllic location transformed what had initially promised to be a pretty depressing day. This was a lesson for us about judging by outward appearances! We should probably have had a little more faith that our God of surprises may have had a part to play in leading us to the right place at the right time.

When we follow Jesus along His own journeys, we find Him not spending time dining in the fancy restaurants of His day, or spending time with the rich and famous. He actually spent a lot of His time visiting the homes of ordinary people, sharing meals with them. Hospitality was important to Jesus, and it was in sharing meals and accepting hospitality that He had many of His most pertinent conversations.

Sometimes we need to value the opportunities to show hospitality, and at other times we need to be grateful for the hospitality shown to us, and recognise the blessings this may bring. The hospitality in that family home in Florence was certainly a great blessing to us on this trip through Italy.

Having had serious reservations on first arriving in Florence, we left with fond memories. We had initially been expecting to find a wonderfully cultured city, but instead discovered something much more authentic. This is one of the joys of riding without hard and fast rules, being able to decide which direction to travel as the journey unfolds, which often leads to the discovery of unexpected treasures hidden within the mystery of the unplanned ride.

One city that did contain a predictable source of culture, though, was Pisa. This is one of the most visited destinations in Italy, and in some respects typifies traditional visions of Italy itself, owing to its iconic leaning tower.

The ride to Pisa was an easy one, and somewhat uneventful. The city was busy, and we were grateful that we were on two wheels. This enabled us to weave effortlessly through the stationary traffic seeking to enter this medieval walled city. We rode through the vast marbled opening to this ancient place, through the narrow and picturesque streets.

We parked opposite an ancient stone church and beneath an adjacent window which had been built into a long, high, stone wall. We collected our gear from the bike and entered a doorway, which had also been recessed into this weather-worn stone wall. Inside, we found an unusually narrow rustic hotel, where we were led to a room overlooking the street. This was slightly away from the very centre, but it was cheap, and it breathed out the wonderful characteristic aroma of the area.

Having settled in, our first stop had to be this famous leaning tower. However, as we approached, even more fascinating than the tower itself was the endless array of camera-laden tourists, capturing their friends struggling with what appeared to be an army of invisible spectres, each one pushing these spectres back with agonisingly disfigured faces, straining to hold these invisible forces from overpowering them, each holding an identical stance, as they pushed back at these foes. It looked like a scene from *The Lord of the Rings*. It wasn't until the tower came into view that these imaginary struggles made sense. There was an obligatory photograph which was expected to be taken, not pushing an invisible spectral force but creating the illusion of holding up the leaning tower. In fact, we both eventually succumbed to this immense peer pressure as we took the stance and saved the tower from falling.

The tower is actually part of a group of ancient Christian buildings encircled within another imposing marbled stone wall. We strolled into this immense courtyard, entering first the perfectly preserved cathedral. A place that had held regular worshippers had now become a haven for tourists, and it felt sad that this once central focus in a previously great city had become a tourist trap. Next to the cathedral stood a large, circular construction, with a winding staircase leading up to a balcony. This great marble building was the cathedral's baptistry, which again had become a haven for tourists. This large building, with its imposing central baptism area, was a far cry from the humble River Jordan where Jesus was baptised by John! In fact, the central focus and symbol of new life had been overshadowed by the actual conduit of water itself.

We finally circled back towards the leaning tower, which also stands next to the cathedral and remains the most famous structure of the three. This large marble tower was initially constructed to stand tall and proud. Its purpose was to be the bell tower for the cathedral. After centuries of attempts, and millions of pounds, they have finally stopped the tower from leaning too far, using cables and drainage. Unfortunately, its intended purpose has been lost, and it has become something of a novelty. The problem was that it didn't have a good foundation and was built on unsuitable ground.

This basic mistake is reminiscent of the one found in a parable of Jesus. Here, within the parable, found in Matthew 7:24-27, Jesus highlights the importance of building one's house on a solid foundation, a foundation of rock. He explains that failure to do this is like building on sand, which shifts and gives way, not dissimilar to what had happened to the leaning tower. He is, of course, using the analogy to represent life, where the solid foundation refers to His life, His words, His example. If we lose sight of this, our faith is in danger of becoming just a novelty, like the leaning tower, which has lost its purpose to originally call people to prayer. A bell tower that has forgotten how to ring, forgotten why it was created, forgotten its roots and traditions, is destined to become impotent.

Foundations are important, and while the tower remains an impressive architectural structure, the immense effort that was expended in rectifying its foundational error, over several centuries, appears to be disproportionately excessive. We decided against purchasing a ticket to climb the tower, and instead headed across a large turfed area, full of meandering tourists following each other from one attraction to another like a flock of stray sheep moving aimlessly through the pastures.

While the tower was the most famous structure of the trio, there was also a fourth building, just as imposing as the previous three. This was the mausoleum, and for me it was the most fascinating building of them all. It held a feeling of loss, full of visitors, but the life had been removed. It was a sort of illustration of the previous three structures, full of activity but with no soul. We entered the building through a pretentiously oversized marble archway, crossing a rectangular open central courtyard surrounded by Roman-style marble pillars. This central area also contained soil brought back from Golgotha in the Holy Land during the Crusades, which gave the mausoleum its name, *Campo Santo*, Holy Ground.

Having crossed this open area, we entered the main section of the mausoleum. It was a cold, atmospheric building, beautifully crafted, again in this imposing marble masonry, but inside feeling somewhat hopeless, holding stone coffins along its wide corridors, along with ancient relics which had also been taken from the Holy Land. It reminded me of Jesus' words to the religious teachers of His time, likening them to outwardly whitewashed tombs, while inside holding only dead bones. Their religiosity hid their spiritual emptiness. In other words, looking outwardly impressive but dead within.[15]

As we walked along the vast hallways, we were drawn to the giant ancient frescoes covering the walls for centuries. Some of these Renaissance frescoes depicted horrific scenes containing demonic beings with pitchforks, tormenting and torturing the poor souls who had been unfortunate enough to find their way to Hell. These souls were drowning in what looked like a burning lake of red, sulphurous liquid. It reminded me of the volcanic river that would have flowed down into Pompeii, wreaking so much devastation. Other images, though, within these frescoes, depicted saints or angels reaching out their hands

---

[15] Matthew 23:27-28.

to rescue the drowning souls. These frescoes, created in the fourteenth and fifteenth centuries, were reminiscent of Dante's *Inferno*, in his *Divine Comedy*. As we walked further in, the frescoes became less dark, depicting various other religious imagery; however, I can't help thinking how those initial chilling images would have affected those who first walked those halls.

The final section of the building led to a large room containing finger bones and other bodily items, encased in ornate containers locked away behind strong safety glass. Apparently, these items, which included numerous body parts, had also been collected from the Holy Land and were retrieved from the likes of the early apostles – or so we were informed. At the time, these items were believed to have the power to heal, among other things. These ideas were drawn from biblical accounts of people being healed as they touched the apostle Paul's handkerchief, as we read in Acts 19:11-12, or to a dead man who was brought to life after making contact with the bones of Elisha the prophet in 2 Kings 13:21, but I am still a little dubious about dismembered body parts having the same effect today!

11
Wanderings and Wrong Turns

Having enjoyed a few days in Pisa, we were heading away from the west coast of Italy and riding towards the eastern regions, where Venice ultimately awaited us. The ride was pleasant, as the sun beamed intensely on our backs, without a cloud in the sky to interrupt its warmth. The roads were open and relaxing as we motored at a leisurely pace. We rode through the outskirts of Venice, following a set of railway lines and the odd train leading us across a long, wide concrete bridge, spanning a large stretch of water which intersected the mainland with the distinctive Venetian waterways. We found that stopping in this main tourist location of Venice was far beyond our means, and so we rode back over the bridge, where we found a fairly cheap but comfortable hotel. Here, we had the best of both worlds, as we were able to relax in a comfortable room, then ride back across the bridge to the ancient parts of Venice.

Things have recently changed, but at that time, when we rode across the water, there was a dedicated and free motorcycle parking area provided at the water's edge. This small area had hundreds of bikes parked up against each other, at various angles, with no methodology for parking, but it seemed to work. We managed to squeeze the bike into a spot, far too small, that had just been vacated near the exit. We then shuffled sideways like a pair of crabs, making our escape from this two-wheeled, abandoned obstacle course.

Once out, we made our way to the beginning of the ancient Venetian canal system. Venice itself lies on the upper edge of the Adriatic Sea, and was formed after the fall of the great Roman Empire. Venice remains one of my favourite destinations, with its ancient and ornate buildings set along narrow, interlinking waterways. On either side of these aquatic streets, we were able to follow the long, winding pathways running alongside unique Venetian homes and inns. Every so often, we would come across small footbridges, which appeared from around various corners. These bridges led us across the canals, and drew us further and deeper into this water-filled rabbit warren. Moving deeper still along these endless waterways, we emerged on the bank of the Adriatic Sea.

The sea stretched across to various islands, with large boats moving to and fro, carrying tourists to the further reaches of these Venetian ports. This central area contained various museums, cafés and restaurants. The food was expensive, so we settled for an Italian beer and a sandwich which we purchased from a local shop, before sitting on the dock of the bay, enjoying watching the comings and goings on the water. We strolled along the water's edge, past an ancient church, and wandered into an art exhibition. We entered a room where various patterned teacups and teapots were suspended among various coloured rabbits, swinging on lengths of wire. We became aware that we had entered the imagination of an extremely disturbed mind, and swiftly escaped this surreal nightmare world.

The walk back to the bike took a little longer than anticipated, as we were now trapped in a water-lined maze, with no idea where we were going. This was not a bad thing initially, as it provided us with an alternative experience of Venice. Here, we once more wandered along the water-filled streets, but this time we were immersed in a graffiti-covered world, which tourists probably normally avoid. However, this eventually led us back in the direction of the bike, as we passed gondolas carrying the wealthy tourists along the scenic stretches of the

Venetian waterways. In fact, we recognised some of these waterways from various movies that had been filmed here.

Walking along this interlinking aquatic maze can be a tangible example of mundane reality. Life is often something of a maze itself, where we attempt to find our way out, not quite sure which direction we should take. We wandered those waterways for a good few hours before finding a way back, as we were led through what may have been some fairly unsafe areas. We could have asked one of the residents for directions at any time, but instead we decided to follow a variety of dead ends. Fortunately, we had the time to meander along those Venetian canals, but in life, this isn't always the case. We often struggle on without any idea of how to escape the traps we find ourselves in. However, when we no longer know which way to turn, when we have exhausted all avenues, God is always ready to guide us back onto the right path.

I have to confess, we didn't pray for guidance as we wandered aimlessly, and we may well have found some direction out of that watery maze if we had taken the time to do so. There are times, however, when our wanderings can be life-giving, even when we don't completely know where they are taking us. It is knowing the difference that is the trick. Those aimless wanderings were just what we needed on the whole, as we were able to enjoy the mystery of the destination and the peace of those water-filled streets.

God is often in our wanderings too, and we were thankful for the time we had, breathing in our surroundings. So, despite being lost, it was certainly worthwhile stopping in Venice, with its unique way of life among the aquatic arteries. However, it was now time to head back to our hotel, and back towards the Alps on our return journey. We left Venice the next morning, partially retracing our steps, until we finally left both sea and city behind. The roads opened up once more, revealing the beautiful countryside that lay on the outskirts of Italy. We were heading now towards Lichtenstein, which we would hit as we passed through Austria. However, before this, we needed to climb the steep Alpine slopes of the Dolomites.

Having left Venice behind, we were now approaching them, and we began our steep ascent through a steady series of hairpin bends. The roads wound through the mountains like a coiled snake, with no barriers to prevent the unsuspecting motorist from plummeting down the sheer drops. However, the bike found a steady rhythm and moved along the pass effortlessly, winding seamlessly through every twist and turn. The initial road was a biker's dream, with the gentle turns that take away the monotony of a straight trajectory. The scenery again was stunning, and became more so as the bike gradually ascended. The sun glistened in a cloudless sky, highlighting the beauty of the imposing Dolomite mountainside. This was the perfect ride! Or apparently so, until we were presented with a seemingly endless series of tight hairpin bends.

The sports bikes moved effortlessly along this tree-lined concertina of tarmac and gravel, but we were two-up on a heavy cruiser with a short steering range. The bike complained at every hairpin incline, with her brakes becoming more ineffective at every turn. The clutch worked harder than it had ever done in its entire life, competing with the bike's desire to accelerate. Finally, after the hard work of manoeuvring this heavy bike, with its low centre of gravity, through these turns, we were relieved to have reached the summit, before heading back down the near-vertical drop.

The journey through the Dolomites is somehow reminiscent of life's journeys. Sometimes they carry us along straight, monotonous roads, leading through the ordinary, predictable and sometimes mundane. At other times, we find ourselves on gentle bends, enjoying every minute of life's wonders, winding through the joys of being alive, of being human. Life often holds variety, though, and sometimes leads us through the hard work of manoeuvring through the hairpins, of moving towards our goals while at the same time holding challenge and excitement. And again, as with a steep descent, we can sometimes feel we have lost control and are heading for disaster. This journey through life is what the writer of Ecclesiastes recognised, when he wrote, 'There is a time for everything, and a season for every activity under the heavens' (Ecclesiastes 3:1). As we negotiated the wide variety of terrain leading through the mountains, including those steep, perilous descents, we felt God's presence and protection throughout. This was certainly important, as we were about to face an equally life-threatening situation caused by technological error.

After overheating the Harley's clutch on the steep incline towards the summit of the Dolomites, we had now begun our near-vertical descent along the sharp, winding Alpine pass. For a short time it was refreshing not to have to over-rev the engine to power us up this steep Italian climb; to be able to look down over the amazing views, to enjoy the harmonious Alpine cowbells and experience the fresh mountain breeze, cooling us down from the blazing heat. However, this was short-lived, as we prepared to take a steep hairpin bend which, as often was the case in the Alps, lacked any walls or barriers to prevent unsuspecting vehicles from launching into the vast mountain air.

As I engaged the front brake, the bike almost shrugged it off, just as easily as it had with the rear. I had lost one of the brakes before, on a ride to Loch Ness, where the rear brake pads completely dislodged from the calliper, but I had never been careless enough to lose both. Now with no rear brake and barely a front, we were accelerating rapidly towards the sheer drop on the edge of this breathtakingly imposing mountain summit.

Frantically attempting to shift down the gears, with little effect on our speed, I noticed a steep natural dirt track to our right, which had probably been created by the local mountain goats. I hit this natural climb, and the speed of the bike carried us up this loose narrow track, but thankfully not over the edge of the mountain. Rather, we eventually headed up the side of a grassy slope, as we eventually joined a bemused Alpine cow, wondering what we were doing in her field. In the meantime, oblivious to the potential danger, Alison, my wife and passenger, asked me why we had taken such a swift detour. I pointed to the overheated brakes, and the hoses, which had now turned to jelly. It then occurred to us that our three-week trip was most probably over.

There was only one thing for it, when stranded on an Italian mountain, besides praying. We opened the bottle of wine we had carried from Italy, along with the shared fragile wine glass, which had been provided during the open-air wine-tasting session in Rimini, several cheeses and some French bread. We then sat enjoying this feast, overlooking the breathtaking views, before planning on contacting a recovery truck.

After enjoying the striking peace of the mountain slope for some time, along with our personalised banquet, we returned to the bike once more. On inspection, the brake hoses had now cooled down, and both brakes were working perfectly again.

It was interesting that even during these potentially life-threatening moments, heading towards the edge of the mountain, there was a sense that God was looking out for us. This had been our feeling during the whole trip, and there was even a tangible feeling of inexplicable peace on that mountaintop as we took in the beauty of God's creation. In fact, it is difficult not to feel in awe in such an environment, and no table at the finest restaurant could have matched that wooden bench, set in the midst of those inspiring views, as we enjoyed our cheese, wine and bread.

This must have been similar to David's experience, as he wrote Psalm 23, looking out over God's creation in the mountains of Israel. The words certainly resonated, especially in relation to the Good Shepherd guiding us along the right paths, and even in the prepared table we had enjoyed on the side of the Dolomite Mountains.

Having enjoyed the opportunity to rest on the summit, with the brakes now working we were once more on our way. We had, however, been struggling with the constant issue of the satnav crashing throughout this trip, owing to its continually dying battery. Having learned from our mistakes on the ride up through France and Switzerland, my wife had developed a system where the passenger would hold the device, in order to intermittently shut it down on long roads to conserve the battery. Because this now meant that I couldn't see the satnav, she independently developed a crude method of translating the various turns, which consisted of a sharp dig in the ribs, indicating left or right. This prototypical navigation method was less than effective, and potentially dangerous for both parties. Therefore the 'bruised rib technique', as it became known, quickly became obsolete. In consultation, it was eventually refined into the more reliable 'arm tap navigation method', which worked well for the remainder of the trip. With this method in play, the seemingly reliable satnav lulled us into a false sense of security, leading us steadily if not reliably through the Dolomites.

We were apparently making good time, and we were riding through even more stunning scenery. We headed down towards a small village, where we approached a small, quaint roundabout surrounded by flowers. The satnav led us off the roundabout and onto a near vertical concrete incline. Despite being steeper than we would have liked, and with the tyres struggling to grip, we were reassured by a reasonably high parallel wall which accompanied us on either side of the initial climb. The satnav confidently reassured us that we were on the right pathway, but as the concrete surface was gradually transformed into a loose gravel track at the same time as the wall fell away, we were left slipping on the shale, devoid of a barrier on either side.

Both wheels now began to slip sideways in the gravel, with nothing to stop us sliding off the edge. It was at this point that we began to have certain trust issues with this satnav. We continued for a couple of yards to the top of the incline, hoping that the gravel would turn into a reasonably solid track. However, the gravel continued as the track plateaued away and turned into an impossible downward incline, reminiscent of steep swimming pool flumes which one finds at water parks.

We were now also faced with a sheer drop to the left of us and a further drop to the right. The steep, loose gravelled track which threatened to lead us into oblivion was now also sloping sideways towards this sheer left-hand-side drop. It was obvious that the satnav had malfunctioned and had led us into one of the most perilous situations we had so far faced.

We had no way of turning round, and were literally stuck between a rock and a hard place. The only way out was to steer the bike backwards along this perilous track towards the concrete pathway. The decision was taken out of our hands, however, as the bike began to slide backwards of its own accord. We were also slipping slightly sideways as the track fell away to our left, in the direction of this sheer drop. If we continued on this trajectory we were following, we would be carried along by the gravel over the edge.

With Alison on the back, I decided on a drastic course of action, leaning the bike and steering towards a wooden post on our right. As the bike slid backwards on the gravel, we banked into the post, where the foot pegs then acted like an anchor. Alison was a little bruised, but we were glad to be alive. As the bike lay on its side, we were now at a loss as to how we would get it back down the lane. The track wasn't suitable for a vehicle, and we couldn't lift it because it would lean back into the incline of the track.

Help came in the form of an irate, aged Italian man, with blackberry-stained hands, shouting at us hysterically. Once he discovered we were English, he angrily said, 'Didn't you see the sign?', pointing to the bottom of the track. The sign apparently read, 'Do not follow satnavs', except it was written in Italian, which was no help to us at all. Incidentally, my wife did helpfully point out several times what a mistake I had made following the satnav up there! Between the three of us, a plan was hatched. I would sit on the bike, applying the brakes and putting it into gear, Alison and the aged Italian man would push the bike from behind to prevent it sliding backwards too quickly, while at the same time Alison would also push from the side to stop it falling into this sheer drop.

I can only imagine what the three of us looked like, clumsily manoeuvring this heavy Harley Davidson. Nevertheless, the bike slid gradually backwards, remaining upright, with some immense effort from Alison, as it finally reached a flat section of pathway by the side of the incline. As the bike rested on its stand, the Italian man and Alison gave each other an enormous hug, both now totally exhausted. We thanked a now more sedate Italian man, with a face as red as the blackberry stains that covered his hands, as he stood there looking like he may not even see the day out.

Our spiritual journey can be like this, and just as perilous, as we can be taken down blind alleys if we follow the wrong voices. In our world we are bombarded with voices claiming to know the way, but at times seeking to draw us into dangerous situations. If we had learned to read the authentic sign, which I suspect this Italian man had erected, we would have known we were following the wrong voice as the satnav drew us onto a highly destructive path. This man not only gave us a clear warning, but also stepped in when we had taken the wrong turn, helping us back onto the safe path.

God is often like this, a voice we can trust, but we need to learn to recognise His voice. When we listen to the wrong voices and take destructive paths, Jesus is still there to help us turn around and point us in the right direction. Once we were on the concrete, we were able to then incrementally turn the bike around, and although the tyres continued to slip, without a passenger I was able to negotiate the incredibly steep descent to the road below.

Having been pointed in the right direction, the remainder of the journey passed without a hitch. The road through Austria was gentle and sweeping, allowing us to enjoy the beautiful scenery as we made steady progress. We made up the time in Germany, where we eventually stopped for the night. In the morning we headed for Belgium, while taking a slight detour into Bruges for something to eat. From Bruges, the ferry was very close, and so we made good time and had a relaxed crossing back into England. The final ride to Leicester was cold and long, and not much fun, but we were eventually glad to be home after an extremely memorable trip together.

Part Three
The Open Roads of Route 66

12

God Rides with Us

It was a warm summer's morning in mid-July 2015, as Alison and I headed for the airport. We had been planning this trip to America for months, having decided to ride the length of Route 66. This ancient highway was established in 1926 and runs from Chicago to Los Angeles, though several sections of the highway have disappeared over time. We were approaching our thirtieth wedding anniversary, which was in the October, and so this was the time to do it. We had again given ourselves three weeks for the trip, and this was one time I really appreciated the long holidays teachers get in the summer.

We had also decided to visit the members of God's Squad while over there, and were kindly offered the use of someone's second house to lodge in – it was being renovated in order to sell. Our plane landed in Chicago, and we were graciously picked up and taken to our hosts' home, where we spent the afternoon getting to know each other better.

There was also an Australian couple staying with us, who had just arrived, and were also members of the bike club. The American and Australian cultures are very different, particularly there in Michigan, as were the political views on the whole, so we realised that two worlds had certainly collided on this weekend. It was particularly interesting when we attended a family barbecue that included some close friends as well as some local bikers. We sat in the front room, drinking a welcome cold beer with our burgers, and enjoying each other's company.

What was noticeable, in comparison to England and Australia, was that the majority were wearing holsters on their belts as we sat talking. Here in Kalamazoo this was nothing unusual, but it certainly gave our Australian visitors some anxiety. While it was certainly interesting, I could see both sides, recognising that America is a very different cultural context to either England or Australia, and we were guests in this country. I was just very grateful to have been able to have got to know some of these guys we shared that time with.

I was reminded of the many times Jesus shared fellowship with the variety of people He bumped into on His own travels. He would often be in rooms filled with the religious elite, Galilean terrorists, corrupt tax collectors or prostitutes, along with down-to-earth guys like the ones I was spending time with in Michigan. Ironically, it was the religious elite that Jesus had the most problems with, and the thing that really concerned Him was their hypocrisy. What was great about spending time with these guys in America was that they were real, honest and easy to talk to. In fact, it has been a pleasure being able to spend more time with some of them on the several other visits I have made.

Although we only had a couple of days on this occasion, we seemed to pack a lot into them. We visited a few bikers, and I enjoyed riding on an old-school Sportster chopper, which handled well.[16] It was also good to be able to ride without the constraints of a helmet, in a state which has no helmet laws, although this didn't particularly resonate with Alison.

It was a real privilege on Sunday morning, before we were due to catch a train to Chicago, to be asked to speak and lead prayers at a low-key morning service called 'Flap Jacks and Jesus', which was attended mainly by bikers. The guys were sitting in a circle around the room. I started by introducing myself. However, before I got any further, a couple of bikers

---

[16] The Sportster is one of the smaller Harley Davidsons, and is often used to build choppers, which are adapted in various ways, often with high handlebars, commonly referred to as ape hangers.

walked in and found seats, greeting everyone in the process. I waited for a moment and began again, repeating what I had just said, when another couple entered and gave their greetings around the room. Again, I waited for a few moments as the banter began to move to and fro. This happened another couple of times until the last ones had finally arrived. By now the room was full of laughter, and it was actually a really good atmosphere, which I found rather refreshing. There was a reality to this meeting, which I have found 'mainstream' meetings can often lose slightly.

I did manage to eventually speak, which was appreciated, and ended in prayer before spending quite a while chatting after the service. It made me think about Jesus' own experiences as He presented His parables and teaching amid the comings and goings in the open air, or while addressing a crowd from a boat.[17] We always assume everyone was standing quietly as they listened to His words, but I wouldn't be surprised if at times He needed to repeat himself, knowing the different types of people who would have been listening to Him.

We boarded the train in Michigan, which would transport us into the heart of Chicago. Once there, we would need to take a bus across town to where we would collect the Harley Davidson we had rented for the journey. Once on the bike we would ride the 2,000 miles of open fields, towns and deserts, which would finally lead us onto the famous pier of Santa Monica, in Southern California, with the magnificent backdrop of the great Pacific Ocean.

On boarding the train, we assumed that this relatively short journey would be fairly uneventful, and this indeed was the case initially. We shuffled along the narrow, carpeted, pulsating corridor, which was bustling with passengers. After running the gauntlet, managing to weave between these unsteady, swaying people, we finally located a couple of seats.

---

[17] Luke 5:1-3.

We weren't sitting down for long before a young man approached me. He looked visibly shaken as he gained my attention, asking if he could talk to me. I climbed out of my seat and stood in the middle of the aisle, where he began by asking me, 'Are you a God-fearing man?' I responded by telling him that I was a Christian, and asked him how I could help. He proceeded to tell me that his sisters were at home on their own, that they were in danger and that they were terrified. He told me that there was a malevolent presence in the house that was causing this terror, and that he believed they were now in serious physical danger. He had just received a phone call telling him that things had got worse, which is why he felt led to speak to me. Looking at him, it was obvious that he was very frightened, and I didn't doubt his account of what was happening.

Some reading this will no doubt be very sceptical; others, on the other hand, will have little trouble believing his story. I myself can often be fairly sceptical. However, on this occasion, I could sense that he was telling the truth, and offered to pray into the situation. We both stood in the middle of the aisle, on this train, heading for Chicago, with me praying for this man and his family for several minutes. When I looked up, I realised that there was a long queue of people lined up behind me, not wanting to disturb our prayers but waiting patiently to get by. I'm not sure I could imagine this happening on the London Underground, but nevertheless on this train to Chicago that is exactly what happened.

It often seems easy to accept the accounts of angels bringing messages of hope in the Bible, protecting men from the flames, ministering to Jesus in the wilderness or opening the prison door in response to the prayers of disciples, as when Peter was supernaturally released from prison.[18] It sometimes bemuses me when the story of Mary believing the angel at the tomb is accepted as so fundamental,[19] but accounts of what this young

---

[18] Daniel 9:20-23; 3:19-26; Matthew 4:11; Acts 12:6-11.
[19] Mark 16:1-7.

man was telling me on this train are often dismissed so easily. Encounters like this remind me that there is both light and darkness, but as the apostle John reminds us, pointing to Jesus, 'The light shines in the darkness, and the darkness has not overcome it' (John 1:5). This is the hope in every dark situation, such as this.

We finally disembarked from the train in Chicago, and after wandering fairly aimlessly around the vicinity of the station, we located a tram that we assumed was heading in our direction. We boarded the tram which, after travelling for ten minutes, came to an abrupt stop at a remote bus station, in what we discovered later was a dangerous part of town. We had seriously miscalculated our bearings, and unbeknown to us at this point, we were in real physical danger ourselves. We stepped down from the safety of the tram and entered a tangibly oppressive atmosphere within a somewhat rundown bus station. The station contained four bus stops on either side of a large rectangular turning area, where the busses would enter and exit the station, and the two sets of stops sat facing each other.

We headed for the furthest bus shelter in order to see whether the bus went to where we needed to be. It was here that I first noticed two large, heavy-set characters wearing black hoodies, reminding me of a couple of old-style gangsters. These two men were actually staring right across from their bus stop, directly at us, with seriously menacing expressions on their faces. We were at the wrong stop, and stepped slowly across to the adjacent shelter. Alarm bells then began to ring in my head as the two men moved in a deliberate manner, almost mirroring our own movements. They again positioned themselves directly opposite us, continuing to stare at us across the expanse.

Although by this point I doubted it, there was a possibility that I was reading too much into this, and scanning the destinations again I realised we still hadn't found our stop. As we moved to the next in line, we were worryingly accompanied once more by our two shadows, who moved in tandem with us, perfectly mimicking our steps. I was pretty sure this was no coincidence, but just to confirm what was happening, we completed our manoeuvres together to the final shelter, which was our bus stop. It now became completely obvious that these two characters were intent on following us. Fortunately, they had remained on the opposite side of the quadrangle. Thankfully, our bus arrived and we mounted the steps to where the driver awaited our tickets. Our two shadows walked straight across from the opposite side to where our bus had stopped, and climbed on behind us.

We found two seats in the middle of the bus while the two men remained at the door we had entered by. As the bus pulled away, the larger of the two walked to where we were sitting, leaning slightly to avoid hitting his head on the roof. He looked us up and down in a slow, deliberate manner, then walked back along the bus to where his friend was standing. After a few words with each other, looking in our direction, he then walked back down the bus and stationed himself at the far exit. We were now completely flanked.

In view of these deliberate movements, I was now preparing myself for trouble, with all kinds of scenarios running through my head. I was more than aware that many Americans in this area carried firearms, either in holsters as in the old Spaghetti Westerns, or concealed on their person. There were numerous possibilities as to why we had been targeted; it could have been that we looked like tourists, or it could have been a territorial thing, as I was wearing my club colours on the back of my leather cut-off. They wouldn't have been able to properly identify these colours from where they had been initially standing.

I was certainly praying as we approached our stop. As we moved towards the rear of the bus where one of them was standing, we were able to depart with neither of the two men following. I'm not sure if they had decided that I may have given them problems, having got a good look at me, or if they were unsure whether I might be carrying a firearm of my own, but I am sure God was looking out for us as we disembarked from that bus.

Feeling a real sense of relief, I said to Alison, 'That was a close one, wasn't it?', to which she replied, 'What was a close one?' I said the fact that those two men who were following us had remained on the bus.

She looked confused. 'I hadn't noticed.'

I said, 'Didn't you see that man who walked across the bus to check us out?'

She said, 'Oh yes, I thought that was bit strange.'

It had been a really tense bus journey, and my wife, who had shared the whole experience with me, had remained blissfully unaware of the potential danger we had been in.

It struck me that faith is a little bit like that bus trip, where we can be oblivious to the whole spiritual world that exists besides our tangible, material existence. I think that is why it isn't until we have a real encounter with God that the world makes sense. The whole message of Christianity is one of realisation of our predicament, and redemption from that by One who came to rescue us. It's a message of hope in a world of danger, a gift of seeing things as they really are, recognising the reality of the unseen as well as the hand that leads us to safety.

The reality is that most people I have met have actually had some type of spiritual experience, but don't always want to acknowledge it, maybe because it will demand interpreting and acting on. On that bus journey I could certainly see the physical interactions, but am certain that God was also clearly acting to lead us to safety, despite one of our party oblivious to the potential danger we were actually in. It certainly helped, as it does on all of my bike trips, to know that God rides with us.

It was now a short walk to pick up the bike, though by now we were seriously overheating, in addition to feeling the need to constantly look over our shoulders. We eventually arrived at the shop and were led to the bike, which was a Harley Electra Glide, along with a rear seat which resembled an armchair. This wasn't my choice of bike, but was part of the conditions laid down by my wife for agreeing to take the trip. There was far too much plastic for my liking, and the bike itself was both heavy and unstable. However, to now be heading off in one piece, with all of our belongings intact, was a real bonus, after the journey we had just taken to get here.

13

Only the Brave

The start of the journey was a little frustrating as we left Chicago amid long lines of slow-moving traffic, but we were soon on the open road travelling across the state of Illinois. The bike had developed a strange rattle, and so we pulled over to check where this was coming from. We soon found out, as we noticed the bike key had jammed in between the steering column.

My own Harley originally shared the ignition with the steering lock, which was located on the steering column. I have since changed this, but originally the key needed to be left in the ignition as the bike was ridden. On newer Harleys, such as the one we were now travelling on, the ignition is on top of the tank and doesn't need the key to start it, as an electronic key fob is merely required to be close to the bike. I had inadvertently left the key in what would have been the ignition on my own Harley, and so the key had vibrated out and subsequently been crushed. Unfortunately, the key also locked all the luggage compartments on the bike, so this now meant that we had to unload the Harley at every stop. We were just fortunate not to have locked the compartments when we set off, otherwise we wouldn't have had access to any of our luggage.

We had only just begun our trip and we were already having trouble. Despite these teething problems, the bike ran smoothly, and we were soon well on the way. We briefly stopped for petrol near Springfield, filling the tank. Alison went across to the cash desk while I looked around the shop.

I asked one of the women behind the counter, 'Is there anywhere you could recommend to eat around here?' She just looked at me, which I thought was pretty rude. I repeated my question in a different way and slightly slower, asking, 'Could you recommend somewhere that would be good to stop for lunch around here?'

By this time Alison had finished paying and was walking over. The woman again just looked at me; then, in a heavy, deep Southern accent she turned her head and shouted into the back, 'Do we have any French speakers?'

Alison intervened at this point, telling her that I wasn't French and that we were both over from England. She then went on to repeat the question I had just asked, in response to which the woman directed us to a diner in town. She had been able to understand Alison perfectly, and the whole thing really didn't make any sense. This was certainly a first for me, being mistaken for a Frenchman by an American woman speaking to me in English. Alison helpfully interjected, 'Don't worry about it – I often find it difficult to understand him, and I'm married to him!'

It reminded me of the Old Testament story of the Tower of Babel, in Genesis 11:1-9, where God prevented the people from understanding each other after they were working together to create something that would stand in opposition to Him. This confusion of language also created a barrier between the people, who could no longer work together, through losing sight of who God was. This division was mended, though, in the New Testament, as the Holy Spirit fell at Pentecost, allowing all language groups to understand the apostle Peter as he told them about Jesus dying for them, being raised, and offering them salvation and reconciliation as they came to the risen Lord.[20]

In that petrol station, it felt like a retelling of the Tower of Babel, where my English language sounded like French to this woman. Thankfully, there was also a retelling of Pentecost, as

---

[20] Acts 2:1-12.

Alison was able to communicate in what sounded like English, bringing reconciliation to the situation!

I wonder sometimes if we don't create our own barriers as Christians, using terminology which only we understand. I wonder whether we need to break down a few barriers by finding ways to make the gospel understood by those around us, without taking the fundamental meaning away, of course, which is the real trick.

We managed to find somewhere to eat in Springfield, and we also discovered the family home of the famous American president, Abraham Lincoln. The house itself was one of many lined up in perfect formation along a leafy lantern-lit street. The houses were constructed of horizontal painted boards on the outside, with what looked like four-by-four timber beams on the inside. The house was laid out with authentic period furniture, with classic leather seating, pale period wallpaper and the very desk Lincoln would have written his speeches from. As we walked back through the front door, peering down this tree-lined street, it was possible to imagine the sound of the horses whinnying as the carriages passed by, heading into town. It was also interesting to just take the time to briefly explore this small town, which was steeped in history.

From here, we rode through fields and farmlands, not entirely different from those we find in England. We stopped at a country diner to eat and got a taste of the American class system. I ordered a steak, and we chatted with the waitress, who appeared to be fascinated with our accents. Here there was no confusion as to whether I was French or not, as she understood every word I said.

Just then, a large pick-up truck sped into the car park, and five large locals spilled out. They entered the diner and sauntered across to a table. In extremely thick Southern accents, they began giving the waitress a really hard time, asking for discounts and generally disrespecting her. I discovered, though, after talking to the waitress, that this was normal behaviour. Unfortunately, there appeared to be an obvious discriminatory hierarchy here, where waitresses sadly found themselves at the bottom. This was some time ago now, and I wonder if things have changed. I am reminded of Jesus' words of challenge and of comfort, when He said, 'But many who are first will be last, and many who are last will be first' (Matthew 19:30). I don't really know where this waitress stood in regard to her faith, but I know Jesus would have been giving this lady time, treating her with respect and telling her about the kingdom of God, where the oppressed who follow Him find comfort.

After this, I was glad to be leaving this small town. We carried on into Missouri, riding through St Louis, and back along the farmlands which ran parallel to the road. We continued on, passing an iconic yellow American Crawford County school bus, where the children were pressing their curious faces against the window. We rode down the road passing yet more fields and crossing narrow ironclad bridges spanning wild, gaping rivers.

We continued to make good progress as we clipped the edge of Kansas before entering Oklahoma. It was here that we heard a deep rumble heading towards us. This was no pack of Harleys; it was a full-blown thunder storm, and we were heading right into it.

As the sky grew dark, long shafts of lightning lit up the vast open sky, like cracks in a window. We had no alternative now but to ride into the storm, with no sign of shelter. The rain hit us hard, as the wind drove large droplets onto my leather cut-off and my now completely numb cheeks. We endured this for the next half hour, before it suddenly subsided, and we were once more riding on a sunlit road.

Isn't life often like that? Our Christian life is often no exception. God didn't promise to make life easy, to remove the storms, but He did promise to ride through them with us, knowing what is on the other side.[21] This time we didn't find ourselves caught in a storm; we made the choice to hit it head

---

[21] John 16:33; Hebrews 13:5.

on, knowing it would be painful. At times we approach these storms of life and need to make the decision to face them head on, knowing Jesus rides with us and will lead us ultimately into the sun.

We continued on, until we noticed a large blue whale looming in the distance, with its mouth wide open as it faced away from a green-tinged pool of water. We pulled in to explore this unusual sight, and were informed that this giant plastic whale was built in the early seventies as an anniversary present for the owner's wife. We also found out that this plastic whale was a famous icon on Route 66, and people would come from miles around to see it and to use the slide, which was incorporated inside the whale's enormous frame, or just to lie on the beach which had been specially created for it. I asked if people still swam there, to which the man replied, 'Only the brave.' It appeared that the lake was now filled with snapping turtles, which could do some serious damage to unsuspecting swimmers. It made me feel slightly nauseous at the thought. This had been a popular place for children to play, years ago, but now the whale had become an obsolete piece of history, a lifeless shell without purpose.

It struck me that this structure stands as a warning to us as Christians, that the structures we create, the liturgies we follow or even the buildings we preserve need to serve the purposes for which they were first designed – to hold the life of the community of believers, to be a place where God is present with His people through His Spirit, where Jesus remains central to all we do. Once our rituals, our focus or our purpose become about the structures themselves, we lose the life that gives them meaning, and we are in danger of becoming as obsolete as this lifeless whale. Keeping our focus on Jesus and allowing our structures to serve Him and bring life into these places will prevent us from becoming obsolete, as we worship together with sincere hearts and a deep love for Christ.

Having left this plastic relic behind, we began the next leg of the journey, which was even more interesting. Here, we passed numerous small-town motorcycle museums containing some rare bikes, mostly Harleys. We also passed through several ghost towns, some of which we stopped off at just to explore the old buildings, which still retained their original character and charm. We passed deserted petrol stations, along with their original petrol pumps. We crossed amazing narrow bridges, which spanned great chasms, and rode along the original concrete-slabbed sections of Route 66. We finally came to the Texan border, leaving this fascinating section of the ride behind us.

We crossed the border into Texas and found another cheap hotel, where two Texan bikers were also booking in. As we began to pay, one of the Texans offered us a discounted room that their friend had booked but had not been able to make. We took them up on the offer and booked into this reasonably priced room. We later joined these extremely loud but interesting Texans for a drink, overlooking a leaf-encased pool, and chatted about biking and the English roads. They recommended a steak house that was famous for serving very good-quality steaks and had been open since the 1960s.

We finally found a table in this busy, themed restaurant, where I ordered a twenty-one-ounce sirloin steak and a pint of beer. The place was full of character and had an excellent atmosphere. We noticed our Texan biker friends, or at least we heard them, but we decided to have a slightly quieter meal, although we could still hear their voices from the adjacent room. Every so often someone would take the seventy-two-ounce steak challenge, which most people failed, but some managed to complete. After enjoying our own steaks, we returned to our hotel, to be ready for the next day's ride.

These chance meetings are significant, and again I do believe God has a hand in coordinating some of these. If we hadn't had met these two, we wouldn't have found the room or spent such a great night at this amazing steak house.

We left the hotel early and headed for the border. However, we noticed to the left of us that there were ten American Cadillac cars buried face down in the desert, looking like precariously positioned multicoloured dominoes. We stopped the bike and wandered over, to find these cars had been covered in graffiti, and that there were a few paint cans lying next to them. For the next twenty minutes, we spray-painted our own designs on these cars and took a picture of our artwork, knowing that when the next tourist arrived, they would most likely redesign our artistic efforts. We then continued on, and as we approached the state border we stopped off at a corner store, where Alison wanted to buy some food and drinks.

As I waited outside with the bike, a large pick-up truck pulled up next to me. A young woman stepped out and entered the store, while her companion, a short, bald man, kitted out in ornate, colourful gear – cowboy hat and over-decorated cowboy boots and spurs – waited on the pavement with me. He introduced himself, telling me that he was a rodeo rider. We chatted for a while and I told him about our bike ride, while he told me about life on the rodeo circuit.

If this conversation wasn't strange enough, as we looked down the street, another pick-up truck screeched to a halt next to a young man who had been walking towards us. A man leaped off the rear of the pick-up with what looked like a roll of brown cardboard in his hands and swung it at the young man's arm. I assumed they were messing about, until the man began running towards us, with his arm swinging uncontrollably by his side like the limb of a rag doll. He then ducked into the store, blood on his jacket.

The passenger from the back of the pick-up then pursued him inside. It was all a little surreal, but this got even stranger. Alison told me that the young man had disappeared into the back, while the owner was shouting at him to hide. Someone was hysterically shouting, 'Call 911, call 911!' The assistant picked up the phone, calling the state police. The man who had broken the young man's arm with such force, with what we later discovered was a sturdy wooden baseball bat, jumped back onto the rear of the truck, and it sped away.

I entered the store to find out what was happening. The rodeo rider with me then picked up a large, round, green melon, held it under his arm like a football and put his hand on the top, rubbing it in a circular motion, before putting his arm on my shoulder, asking Alison to take a picture of us both. I'm not sure why, but I still have the picture! The woman from the store asked us if we had seen what happened. I told her that we had, and she instructed us to wait around for the police, who would want to question us and get a statement, but we were on the bike and out of there. The last thing I wanted was a Texan police officer questioning me, knowing that they didn't particularly like bikers.

We quickly headed for the border, where we stopped briefly as I put my helmet on (Alison wore hers all the time), which hadn't been compulsory in Texas but was across the state line. We had been informed that the police often sat on the border waiting for bikers who had forgotten to replace their helmets. Sure enough, as we crossed the state line, two police officers were sitting there in a police car, and I was both relieved and sorry at the same time to be leaving Texas.

14
Moving On

We now entered New Mexico, and we decided to take a fifty-mile detour from Route 66 into Santa Fe. These were some of the best rides of the whole trip, as narrow roads swept gracefully through the desert. We decided to stop here for the night, finding another cheap hotel. The town had real character, and had the sounds and feel of an old Mexican village. It was actually founded as a Spanish colony and is the capital city of New Mexico. We enjoyed the relaxing atmosphere as we sat out overlooking the immensity of the desert.

However, the real destination I was eager to visit was Madrid, which was made famous by the film *Wild Hogs* and was actually a fairly isolated small town. We set off early, and again the roads were amazing, being barely wide enough for two cars. These narrow roads crossed dried-up riverbeds as they wove gently through picturesque mountainsides, and contained some exhilarating corners. The sun crept above the mountain range as we approached Madrid, and we parked up not far from a place which was a bar at the centre of the final action scenes in the film, but was actually a souvenir shop.

We wandered along the main street and stopped in an actual bar. This was a fairly pleasant place, with live music and a comfortable atmosphere. We found a table and relaxed for lunch with a small glass of low-strength American lager. On the way out, another biker mentioned that this town had zero-alcohol limits, so we stuck to soft drinks after this. These types of inconsistencies between state laws, or even town regulations, can catch you out, as one town may demand the wearing of helmets, disallow filtering between traffic or even, bizarrely, demand the compulsory carrying of firearms, as with Kennesaw, Georgia. Other states or towns will have completely opposite regulations, which sometimes makes riding across state lines interesting.

We spent a couple of hours exploring the area, before climbing back on the bike. Again, we rode along the amazing narrow winding roads, through more spectacular desert scenery. However, we were ten minutes down the road when the intensity of blue flashing lights signalled the arrival of a fairly large police vehicle. As it came tearing around a narrow corner, just before it passed extremely close to the bike, it unnervingly flashed its bright halogen headlights straight at us. This enforcement vehicle could have been driving to any manner of emergency, and we will never know exactly what his rush was, but it did make me a little paranoid, and I was certainly glad these roads were too narrow for a vehicle to do a U-turn. Nevertheless, we continued along these breathtaking roads until we once more reached Route 66, making our way swiftly to Albuquerque.

As we continued through New Mexico, we passed more deserted ghost towns that lay along these great desert roads. We finally reached Albuquerque, where the TV series *Breaking Bad* had been filmed, as well as the majority of the scenes from *Wild Hogs*. I was interested to see the area, having enjoyed the TV series, even though we couldn't find the house where some of the action happened. It was interesting to see the actual desert where much of the series was filmed, and it was possible to recreate the scenes in our minds as we looked out on this unforgiving arid expanse.

Having ridden around for a while, we then needed to find a place to stop for the night. We again found somewhere cheap to stay, which was nothing special but did the job.

We decided to have a walk, in order to explore some of the town. We walked into a bar, which was frequented by American veterans, and it felt like we had walked into the scene of a film. The bar fell silent as the atmosphere took on a hostile feel. We ordered a couple of drinks, but it was obvious we were not welcome in this place as we were handed two bottles of beer. We drank them quickly. As we stepped through the door, however, we bumped into a biker who had just pulled up and was now climbing off his Harley.

This biker was part of a local back patch bike club, and was actually the doorman at this establishment. He greeted us as we began to exit, and I asked him about his bike. I told him that I had travelled from England and that I was a member of a Christian bike club over there. It was interesting how we seemed to hit it off, and got into a relatively deep conversation, partly about faith. I really can't remember how it came about, but for some reason he told me that he had been adopted. When I told him that I had been adopted too, he then gave me a great hug and kissed me on the neck, to Alison's bemusement. He entered the bar and spoke to the bartender, whose attitude immediately changed.

I don't know if it was the fact that we were both bikers, that I was a Christian or that he had felt some empathy at sharing a similar experience, but I walked into a hostile bar and left as a friend. I am convinced God had led me into that conversation, and even though I didn't have a clue why this biker had been so happy to have met me, I hoped there had been some encouragement in our conversation.

Having now filled up and found somewhere to eat, we made a brief stop in Winslow. This particular town was made famous by the hit song 'Take it Easy'. The song was written by Jackson Browne and Glenn Frey, who was also the lead singer of the Eagles. With this iconic song in our heads, we pulled up next to the famous statue which stands on a corner of Winslow, having been erected in memory of the song. We climbed off the bike and took the obligatory pictures.

We then wandered along the main street, which had little of interest, and entered the one place that appeared to be open, which was a small coffee shop. We asked them if they were still serving, which they were. We ordered a coffee and sat down to relax for a while. As we drank our coffee, the waitresses began to clear the tables around us, as if we weren't there, dusting the tables off and putting the chairs up around us. They then began to clear our table completely, taking away the sugar, spoons and serviettes. It was obvious that they were wanting to close early, and that we were just an inconvenience to them.

When I reflected on how I felt about the town, I thought perhaps they were living on past glories, which faded with each generation who failed to recognise the ageing song. Our faith walk can be a little like that, grounded on a decision we made in the past, without moving on with God into the things He has for us now. Our faith journey can be like travelling on an escalator, where, if we are standing still, we are actually going backwards. It is certainly important to hold on to our early decisions, to remember how God has worked in the past, but if that is where we stop, we will lose sight of where He is leading us in the present.

I often find it interesting, as a vicar, when people tell me that they were baptised in the church or got married there, and this seems to validate their Christian faith for them. It is great to hear people sharing these things, but if we never move beyond our early baptism into a life spent with Jesus at the centre of our lives, we miss so much that He has for us. It is the same as attending church only at Christmas; it's great – but it is a little like taking a Harley for its MOT once a year and thinking that this makes us a biker. It takes more than owning a bike and taking it to a garage to be a biker; it is the love of riding, the passion for bikes which becomes a part of everyday life, part of our identity in some respects. Living as a Christian is exactly the same, living out this life every day with a passion for God. We cannot live on past experiences. Instead we need to journey with God every day, in an authentic faith journey. We left that town, having found a landmark in time, and then moved on in order to discover where God may be leading us in this very real and exciting present.

Having left one landmark in time, we were now heading twenty-five miles across the desert to visit another. Unlike the Grand Canyon, this next landmark was privately owned, and for me it was well worth the five-mile diversion from Route 66. This was the sight of the massive Barringer Meteor Crater. Apparently, it is not uncommon for meteors to strike the earth's atmosphere, but they often disintegrate as they strike the earth's upper protective layer. Some meteors get through, but make little impact on our planet. This was one of the exceptions, as it created a crater that was more than 4,000 feet across, with an original depth of 750 feet. Having been filled in slightly by time, it is still 550 feet deep.

The meteor that caused this crater most likely had a diameter of around 150 feet, and it was made of a metallic substance. The immense impact was also considered to have been equivalent to the force of 20 million tons of high explosives.[22] We were actually able to see a fragment of the meteor at the visitors centre next to the crater. The crater was incredible, and there were observation platforms set around the edge where it was possible to look deep into it. There was a small hut built in the centre that was barely visible to the human eye from this height, and which gave a good impression of just how huge this crater was. It was possible to walk down into the crater's base, although we didn't have the time or the energy to.

Standing at the edge, my mind was drawn towards the vastness of space, from where this meteor arrived. Looking into the enormity of this crater drew my thoughts towards the One who created not only this meteor, but also the very planet it made contact with. In considering the power that this meteor demonstrated as it came crashing into earth, I considered the

---

[22] See Dean Smith, *The Meteor Crater Story* (Winslow, AZ: Meteor Crater Enterprises, 1996), pp 9-11.

immense power of the One who set it on its path through the vastness of space. And although He held this immense power in His hands, He also entered our world in vulnerability as a child in Bethlehem, and in vulnerability died for us in Jerusalem. It was this same One who created all we see and all we can ever imagine, the same One who placed the stars into space and worlds into being.

We continued our journey through Arizona, passing the famous Painted Desert, a wonder of the natural world, and a petrified forest. This led us to an even greater expression of God's creative power, within the Grand Canyon itself.

15

A Far Better Option

As we approached the Grand Canyon, we were faced with miles of stationary traffic, and while an air-conditioned car may well be a suitable environment to park for a while, we wouldn't have lasted long on the bike in that heat. We decided to filter through the lines of four-by-fours and high-sided vehicles, which is exactly what we would have done in England. It wasn't easy, though, as the weight of an armchair complete with occupant was threatening to destabilise the bike, and was eager to tip us over as we moved through at extremely low speeds.

We also hadn't fully appreciated just how long this queue of traffic was; it appeared to be unending as we rode on for more than twenty minutes. As we finally neared the front, several people were shouting what appeared to be abuse through their windows, and a couple of large vehicles actually tried to ram us off the road, making us swerve as we passed by, narrowly missing several mirrors. The thought also occurred to us that these guys carried guns, and we were easy targets for an unstable individual who had been sent over the edge by the heat.

As we approached the gates, which began to open before us, we understood the frustration. We discovered that the national park had been shut for hours because of the unusually high volume of visitors, along with the lack of parking spaces, and this queue had literally stretched for miles without moving for more than three hours. As we approached the front, they had just that minute opened the park. We could see how frustrating this must have been to those who had sat for hours waiting near the front of this queue, just to have a couple of bikers muscling in. We also hadn't appreciated that filtering in this state was illegal, which would have added to their annoyance. Despite all of this, though, God's timing was perfect, and we actually rolled into this national park barely needing to stop.

We pulled up next to the canyon, at Mather Point. The views were magnificent, and the immensity of the canyon is inexplicable – a very fine line beneath was actually a mighty river that runs through the canyon. We wandered down a track which, if we had continued, would have led to the base of the canyon hours later. As we turned a corner, there was a young woman standing on one leg, reaching out into oblivion, while her boyfriend took her picture. Some of these guys are completely reckless, and I wonder how many of them have actually fallen from this height.

If I hadn't arrived with a belief in a creative God, this view couldn't have failed to convince me. It was hard to imagine what vast and unimaginable creativity God must possess. I really cannot comprehend how something so magnificent, something so awe-inspiring that cries out and demands our total attention, could fail to draw our minds to our Creator. In fact, there is no reason why we should naturally gain pleasure from a large chasm of rock, but I believe that we have been given the gift to be able to appreciate the beauty within creation, and to have our breath taken away at such wondrous sights as these.

We climbed onto a small shuttle bus, which took us further into the park and allowed us to take in some alternative views of this great canyon. Here, we also experienced the ruthless effectiveness of the American police force. A man had boarded this shuttle bus with his family at the same time as us, and for some reason was getting frustrated with the female driver. He didn't appear to be causing too much trouble, but was certainly disgruntled at something, so much so that he questioned the driver from his seat. The next thing we knew was that, without warning, the doors were automatically locked and the shuttle pulled over. Two police officers then boarded it, pulled the man to his feet, handcuffed him and led him away into a police car, followed by his whole family. I had never seen anything like it! If this were to happen in England, the bus services would be emptied in the course of a few hours. This appeared to be zero tolerance on steroids.

On leaving the Grand Canyon, we decided to find a hotel, both to spend the night and in order to relax, having covered a lot of ground over the previous couple of days. As we entered the town of Seligman, our eyes were drawn to three Wild West-style houses to the left, which in Westerns typically contained certain career ladies who often stood on balconies waving at customers. As we came closer to the three wooden houses, sure enough, there were seven ladies dressed for business, standing motionless as they watched us entering the town. As we approached, they didn't make a move, but continued staring down at the street. We finally realised why they were so focused: each one was a quirkily dressed mannequin. They had been set up in historical dress, and two of them stood beside a cowboy leaning out of a window. The other mannequins resembled a couple of ladies who were accompanying a 1920s Chicago gangster, as well as a group of American hipsters.

As we rode through, we noticed that there were several rusted classic cars and trucks which had been left by the early travellers along this route. These sorts of cars could often be observed abandoned in the desert, often bereft of wheels and interiors. Besides the curiosities, we located an interesting hotel, in which every room had a different theme. We decided to stop the night in the John Wayne room, seeing as we were stopping in a town with a Wild West feel to it. The owner was excited to let us know that many famous people had stayed in the hotel and related to us the way the town had been dying, as travellers didn't stop there. However, the town barber decided to rejuvenate the town by creating items of interest, which was why travellers were greeted by this row of mannequins on the way through. It certainly worked, as it caught our attention.

These mannequins and this town barber made me think about the way the world often focuses on the ones who appear to have the loudest voices, the ones who put themselves forward, who raise themselves up, who love the limelight.

We often overlook the ones who actually might have something to say, the quiet ones, the humble. When Israel wanted a king, to be like all the surrounding nations, God initially presented them with Saul, a man taller than all the rest, a man with a big personality, and a charismatic figure.[23] However, things eventually went seriously wrong for Saul, before David, the man God had chosen to replace Saul, was revealed.[24] In contrast, David was a humble shepherd, overlooked by his family, living in the fields with the sheep. Yet this humble shepherd became one of the greatest kings Israel had ever seen, with a heart focused on God, loved by his people, and who killed the giant Goliath with a slingshot.[25]

God values the humble, the ones with a heart for Him, not necessarily the loudest. When we entered that town, our eyes were drawn to those figures, standing on their pedestals, high above the street. However, they had nothing to say; they were empty inside, all show, whereas the one who actually transformed the lives of the people within that town was a humble barber. We need to listen to the quiet voices, to the overlooked, and even to the voices on the fringe, those such as David.

We enjoyed our time in that town, and sat outside one fascinating shop, which had a graffitied 1920s car permanently parked outside. Next to the car stood two historic Route 66 petrol pumps, and a seating area where it was possible to order an American ale. We ordered a couple of beers, and relaxed in this unique atmosphere. Another couple sitting at the table next to us asked us where we had come from. We told them that we

---

[23] 1 Samuel 8:5-9; 9:2.

[24] 1 Samuel 13:13-14.

[25] 1 Samuel 17:12-51.

were from England, and had travelled from Chicago. They were relatively local, so I asked them if there was anything to be aware of travelling to Las Vegas. The man told me that he worked for the local sheriff's department, and warned us to ride well within the speed limits as we passed through the reservations, as they have their own unique enforcement officers. He warned us that they are particularly on the lookout for bikers who travel slightly too fast, in order to give them heavy on-the-spot fines, which they often take a cut from. He also warned us to stay clear of a particular town which was extremely unsafe, though, unfortunately, we were inadvertently about to stop in that very place.

We travelled along Route 66 once more, passing the famous original 'Burma-Shave' signs that were spread along the route, containing various lines of rhyme about the benefits of using this particular wet shaver. This was highly entertaining and passed the time. Then we stopped for petrol, as well as something to eat. We walked towards the door, where a young man in a cut-off had been watching us too closely. I had a bad feeling about this, and asked him if he was part of a bike club. He told me that he was hanging around for the local bike club in this town. By this he meant that he was taking the early steps to join this local back patch bike club. I felt prompted to look back as we walked on, to see him immediately on his phone; I was certain he would be informing his club that another back patch biker was encroaching on their territory, even if I was a Christian.

We decided to forget the food and get out of there, which was a good idea, as we noticed on the way out that we had unintentionally ventured into the one town that we were warned against the day before. If I hadn't been prompted to look round at that point, we would have probably stayed, with what I am sure would have been some dire consequences. I do think that God prompted me to look round at just the right time, as He so often does in these circumstances, even though I could never prove that. God does thankfully work in some unusual ways.

After a fascinating stay in Seligman, we were now well on our way to Vegas. We took it steady riding through the reservations, particularly after the previous warnings. Riding at slower speeds meant that we noticed a sign for a 'Native American Cultural Centre'. This sounded like it could be an interesting visit, even if it might be slightly commercial. This turned out to be one of the highlights of the trip. We pulled up outside and then entered the centre, expecting exhibits and information sheets, along with a ticket kiosk. However, we discovered that this wasn't actually a tourist exhibition, but was a centre where the young people of this particular reservation came to learn their tribal traditions.

Far from being turned away, we were welcomed in and offered a cup of coffee and a biscuit. We were taken to a meeting room where one of the experts on their tribe had just been teaching. He was eager to hear about life in England, and was also pleased to hear that I was a teacher with a background in religion. I hadn't expected the next conversation, however, as he asked me what town we were from. I explained that we were from Leicester, and he went on to ask me about the recent discovery of King Richard III. Interestingly enough, I had just been on a course for school teachers, led by one of the professors who had helped discover King Richard in a local car park, ironically buried beneath a large letter 'R'.

Following a fascinating conversation, we were asked if we would like a tour, for which we were extremely grateful. We were shown around the centre, meeting several young people, and it was a real insight into another culture.

Having had the chance to see the centre, we were then invited to watch a traditional tribal dance that was being taught outside. We were introduced to the teacher, who explained that they were learning a local traditional dance called the 'Bird Dance'. While some of the Native American dances can hold alternative spiritual significance, which we would not have been comfortable with, this 'Bird Dance' was historically rooted. It was a way of recalling the distant journeys that the tribe had made to find their home, using the imagery of a bird's flight.

As they prepared for the dance, the teacher sat in the middle of a line of six young people of various ages. Four of the young people were each holding a maraca, which they shook in time to the song and which would later accompany the dance. We were again asked if we would like to see the young people perform the 'Bird Dance', which we took as a real privilege. One of the young people was delighted that we wanted to watch them, explaining how hard he had worked at getting it right.

The dance began with the young people sitting, as they began to chant the lyrics, again to the rhythm of the maracas. Three of the young people then stood up and began to perform the dance, moving to and fro, with clear movements as they chanted. This was reminiscent of some of the old film clips, but had an authenticity. The young man who had been excited that we wanted to watch them was taking it extremely seriously and with real enthusiasm, wanting to get it right, as he turned to look at us every so often.

While all the young people spoke English, the chanting was presented in their traditional tongue. We had watched more polished choreography in the past, with what had been presented as authentic costumes, but there is always a sense that performances, even those that are drawn from traditional roots, are designed for the tourists. Here, there was none of this; instead, it was a simply performed traditional dance, and was designed to help the young people of that tribe preserve their heritage and history as they recalled the journeys of their tribe across the desert.

This concept of authenticity drew my thoughts to my own traditions and history within my Christian faith. While the simplicity and authenticity of this dance had a purely historical context, I sometimes wonder if our worship can become too professional, too polished, which brings the danger of being performance-driven. I have been considering recently whether we need to go back to the simplicity of worship, looking back at some of the old hymns that form part of our Christian traditions, appreciating the sound doctrine and truths contained within them. They recall our deep Christian history, reminding us of who God is; they draw on our credal and biblical foundations, and help us worship our Trinitarian God. I would not want to jettison the newer expressions of worship, the new songs that help us express our love for God, but we need to be careful we don't also jettison our foundations which provide real depth of expression with authenticity.

We finally left the reservation with valuable memories, as we continued to head for Vegas.

During our planning phase for this tour, we had considered joining a group led by a tour guide, who would possess local knowledge and who would take the group to all the famous places along Route 66. In following our own course, we missed certain attractions worth seeing, we bypassed interesting museums that the tour guides would visit, and we sometimes found ourselves riding into dangerous places that the guides would avoid. However, we wouldn't have had the time to divert, to explore new places or to engage with the lives of real people. If we had been part of a guided tour, we would have ridden straight past this cultural centre, we would have missed experiencing this amazingly authentic performance and being able to find out about other people's experiences.

As we rode across America, we did actually intersect a guided tour on several occasions. On one occasion we were sitting in a historical café when the group descended on us, but it was clear they had a tight schedule to follow. The group came and went as we relaxed in this café, with its wall lined with historic photographs and posters depicting the old route. We passed the group again in a busy town, as they were getting ready to book into a fairly characterless guesthouse; we rode further on, finding a relatively small, historic hotel, which gave us a fascinating glimpse into 1920s living with its enormous stone walk-in fireplace as a central feature. On the sides were two parallel curved stairways, laid with red carpet, which led up to the main bedrooms. Unfortunately, we were unable to afford to stay in any of these rooms, and ended up stopping in one of the sets of outside rooms, which was actually quite pleasant, and meant that we could also make use of the main hotel's amazing 1920s lounge. If we had been travelling with a group, we would have missed stopping in this amazing place.

On another particular intersection, we just missed the group as they were leaving a café made famous by the Disney cartoon film, *Cars*. We entered the café and were greeted by a lady who gave an incredibly fast and carefully choreographed speech, which she obviously gave to all the customers.

While a tour would have been interesting, I doubt it would have brought us into contact with half of the fascinating people we met, or taken us into half of the rough and ready places we visited. We wouldn't have met people like the rodeo rider and, more importantly, we would have missed that wonderful bird dance. Visiting the tourist traps would have been entertaining, but I much prefer engaging with real people.

These diverse routes with either a tour guide or riding solo both brought us to the same destination. We both began in Chicago and would end up in Santa Monica in California. However, as is so important in life, the journey was very different. My favourite poem is 'The Road Not Taken', by Robert Frost,[26] which expresses this sentiment well. Here, Frost narrates the story of a traveller taking a pleasant walk along a path leading through a wood, before coming to a fork. He took the less worn of the two, considering later that this had been the better choice. Just like Robert Frost's traveller, we definitely took the road that was not as popular, and that too proved to be the far better option.

---

[26] See www.poemhunter.com/poem/the-road-not-taken (accessed 4th October 2023).

16
Twists and Turns

As we loaded up the bike, having experienced some of the most amazing natural phenomena we had ever seen, and having been awestruck by the immensity of the canyon which no camera can do justice to, we headed on to Las Vegas, which was actually a detour in our journey. Vegas itself was more than 100 miles away, and we were slightly late leaving. What this meant, though, was that we would be travelling in the heat of the desert sun at its hottest point. As we approached the desert road, we felt like we had been placed in a preheated oven, as we began to slowly cook.

We had already drunk our water reserves, and so made use of the last convenience store before we started our journey into the desert. We had been thinking that Las Vegas may be an expensive place anyway, and so we decided to stock up on water for the couple of days we were there. We bought a massive five-gallon rectangular container of ice-cold spring water, which just about fitted on the sizeable rack of the bike, and which was designed to keep a family going for several weeks. As we began our ride through the desert and the heat became unbearable, we made several stops for water, gasping for what was now a hot-water tank. The journey would have been a pleasant one if we had taken it in one of the air-conditioned cars that passed by every so often.

Our black T-shirts and my leather cut-off were not helping with the heat, as they now felt as though they had been placed on top of a fireguard. I was reminded of the programmes where people cook eggs on the roads in these desert regions, and this road was at a perfect temperature for this. We stopped for one more water break, realising we had now drunk gallons of water in less than half an hour, and it was clear we were not going to make Las Vegas without more water. It seemed hopeless, and we were aware that people have actually died of dehydration in this place, and in fact this ran adjacent to Death Valley... the name says it all.

Just as we were losing hope, we noticed a sign for the world-famous Hoover Dam, which we now aimed for. We were actually only thirty miles away from civilisation and the edge of Las Vegas, but at that moment it might as well have been 300 miles. As we pulled into a complex which led to the dam, we were more interested in finding water than observing the technological marvel, and thankfully we managed to locate a fountain, spending some time guzzling this water before finally taking a walk to the dam itself.

Sometimes we fail to recognise how precious a simple glass of water can be, as we take for granted the ample supply we find living in a country where water is plentiful. The problem with riding through this desert was that the water we were carrying didn't satisfy. No sooner had we stopped to drink than we were once again thirsty, as the immense heat immediately robbed the moisture from our bodies.

Jesus talks about this constant thirst in a conversation with a woman at a well, in another dry and arid place. Having asked her for water, He notes that it will not ultimately quench a person's thirst, and they will continue to be thirsty. This was something that had become very real to us at this point in the desert. However, Jesus tells the woman that He has water that will quench a person's thirst permanently. Jesus tells her, 'Indeed, the water I give them will become in them a spring of water welling up to eternal life' (John 4:14). It is almost like this cold, refreshing water fountain that we were now drinking from, with an endless supply of water – if it had been able to eternally quench our thirsts. Jesus made it clear that this water is available to all.

I can relate to spiritual thirst, but I can also relate to this thirst-quenching living water which has become as precious to me as the water in that desert was to us that day. Jesus was referring to the Holy Spirit, who leads, guides and brings eternal peace into our hearts, living water in the midst of a desert, literally bringing eternal life.

Having temporarily quenched our thirst, we took a trip around the Hoover Dam, which was named after the famous United States president of the same name. Many thousands of workers were involved in the dam's construction, and the city of Boulder was originally designed for these workers. As well as holding a massive water reserve, the dam creates great amounts of electricity as the falling water rotates the enormous turbines to power the equally mammoth generators. It is possible to take a trip down into the depth of these generators, but we really had to continue on our journey to Vegas. We did enjoy wandering around this amazing structure, looking down at the great river beneath, as well as taking in the enormity of the construction that provided the surrounding areas with water.

Having cooled off slightly, and having managed to buy more water, we headed towards Las Vegas. However, we had neglected to book a room for the night, assuming there would be plenty of cheap hotels in the city. We quickly found out that they weren't the safest places to stop, neither for us nor for the bike. We found ourselves riding into the outskirts of the city, where men and women were curled up against walls or wandering aimlessly with trolleys and tattered clothing. We had found the cracks in this place, the areas where poverty was rife. This was the hidden population, the outcasts living on the fringes of an over-affluent town, and there was little we could do to help.

We pulled up in a local hamburger outlet, intending to buy something to eat but, looking around, we quickly realised this was a bad idea, so we continued back to the main strip. The street was lined with perfectly presented themed hotels, in the shape of circus tents, or mimicking the Eiffel Tower. There was an Egyptian sphynx, as well as the famous Caesars Palace, which we wandered over to later on. We managed to find a less expensive place, but discovered that all the hotels were interconnected.

Our room was basic but it suited our needs, and there was somewhere to park the Harley for the night. We changed out of our bike gear, then had a much-needed shower and a cup of coffee. We stepped out of our room and into a corridor leading to a wide, carpeted hall, surrounded by one-armed bandit slot machines. I don't as a rule gamble, but on this occasion, here in Vegas, I decided to risk it. These machines gave four spins for a dollar, which I didn't want to spend, so I decided to insert a quarter for one spin. I pushed the coin into the slot with some force, at which the alarms sounded, the machine began to flash and, as we ducked out of the way, several heavy-set security men approached at pace. What I hadn't realised was that while it was a quarter for a spin in theory, the machines only took notes, so I had now jammed up this expensive machine. This taught me a lesson, and that was the last time I attempted to gamble.

These machines were obviously intended to be hypnotic. People sat on stools, feeding these ever-hungry slotted mouths with paper, as the busy, immaculately dressed staff provided them with endless complimentary drinks. Moving on, there were the more serious games, of roulette or poker, where people must have been spending hundreds of dollars. My attempt at forcing this quarter into the machine didn't exactly make me a big spender!

As we continued down these long corridors, we finally came to an escalator, which led onto the street. Here, there were magicians, street performers and people wearing all manner of weird and wonderful costumes. We crossed the road to where a giant Harley Davidson was positioned to look as though it had crashed into the wall of a Harley-themed café. Inside, there were some interesting bikes, including a recreation of the famous *Easy Rider* chopper, which had appeared in the film.

After enjoying browsing the shop, and relaxing with a coffee, we made our way back along the interconnecting hotel corridors, finally arriving at Caesars Palace. This was an impressive hotel, filled with ancient Roman pillars, marble fountains and a space that emulated the inner area of the famous Colosseum. Beyond the Ancient Roman layout there were the predictable bars and restaurants.

As I looked at one of these impressive pillars, I gave it a tap, and the whole thing was made of hollow plastic. It all looked impressive on the surface but was in fact empty inside, without substance. In some respects, this summed up Vegas: it was a fascinating place to visit, but to me it was a soulless, empty city with no real substance, an escape from reality for many. While I found the atmosphere fascinating, it really upset Alison as she watched this utter excess of money and self-indulgent luxury, while just beyond the boundaries there were people sleeping in the streets.

This reminded me of one of Jesus' parables of a rich man who lived in luxury, while a poor man called Lazarus sat starving outside his gates. In Luke 16:19-31, Jesus related how the rich man, who had made no effort to help Lazarus and had lived purely for himself, died and went to Hades, but when Lazarus died, he was lifted up to a place of comfort. Jesus said in life the rich man had 'good things' (v25), while Lazarus had suffered, and now things were turned upside down. As I considered those homeless men and women, who were in some sense outside the gates of this opulent place, I couldn't help but see a real comparison. In the end, Vegas was a mirage, smoke and mirrors, with no real substance, just like those hollow, painted pillars.

We prepared the Harley a little earlier for our return journey from Vegas, in order to avoid the intense heat of the Mojave Desert, which we had experienced on the way there. We followed the road back to Route 66, where we would ride one of the most amazing sections of this historic highway. While the majority of roads had been relatively straight, this narrow desert section of old Route 66 followed a flowing trajectory, with some of the most beautiful views we had experienced so far. The surroundings were rugged and unspoilt, as the road clung to the side of the mountain and fell away towards the desert, traced only by three thin strands of wire that almost passed for a barrier. These views would have been identical to the ones the early travellers would have experienced as they followed the route decades before.

As we headed along the initial section, we hit a sandstorm, which picked up great quantities of fine dry sand from the surrounding desert and launched it towards us with force. We quickly pulled off the road, finding refuge in a small-town convenience store. This brief sandstorm didn't last long, but it had acted like a sandblaster, removing some of the surface from my leather cut-off and leaving tiny indentations. We emerged from the store to a different world, as the sun lit up the vastness of the desert once more, restoring its original beauty.

We sometimes find ourselves engulfed in our own spiritual sandstorms, unable to see the reality of a sunlit plain. It is in these moments that we need to remember the light hasn't been removed; it is just that we are prevented from experiencing it as we travel through the hidden patches. While these storms may leave their mark, God is able to hold us through them and reveal once more the reality that He hasn't left us.

We continued along the winding mountain track and entered a town called Oatman. Here, we rode slowly into another world, where a mock gunfight was being re-enacted for the amusement of tourists. However, it wasn't the guns that forced us to stop, but a donkey standing defiantly in our path. It reminded me of the Old Testament story of Balaam's donkey in Numbers 22, which refused to take him along the road he shouldn't have been taking in the first place. The donkey saw an angel standing with raised sword in hand, unseen by Balaam and ready to oppose him. God then allowed the donkey to speak to Balaam;

the donkey saved his life by preventing him from taking a route contrary to God's instructions. Balaam then repented, and as so often is the case when we come clean with God, God forgave him and saved him from these consequences, allowing him to see the reality of the situation.

While at times we can find ourselves moving within a desert storm, on other occasions we can be in peril from our own choices. But again God often gives us the opportunity to turn round, or to make different choices, as Balaam did. I was certainly glad that this particular donkey hadn't begun to talk to me as it prevented us from riding into this local gunfight. As the show ended and the gunslingers cleared the street, we were permitted to continue on our journey. We hit a couple of really exhilarating bends, before making contact with a stretch of newly gravelled road, which both slowed us down and enabled us to enjoy the last of this spectacular desert scenery.

After several more twists and turns we finally intersected the highway leading to California. We eventually managed to negotiate the heavy Californian traffic and made it to Santa Monica, riding onto the pier, which marked the end of Route 66. The last couple of days were then spent relaxing on this iconic beach before flying to Chicago, where we would catch our plane home. God had been faithful throughout the whole trip, and we had certainly been aware of His intervention on more than one occasion.

Part 4
Snowbound in America

17

A Close Call

It was five years later when I returned to Michigan, this time the middle of January 2020, and while I expected some cold weather, I wasn't entirely prepared for the deep snow I experienced. What this meant was that I was unable to ride, and instead travelled extensively in large, black four-by-four vehicles with engines the size of small jet planes. On this visit I was travelling with another member of God's Squad in order to spend time with the members of the Michigan God's Squad chapter and also to visit other bikers in the area. We were here for just over a week, and I was also due to preach on one Sunday morning, but more of that later.

After a long flight to Chicago, I met the member from the UK who I would be travelling with, and we made our way through the snow in a small hire car to Michigan and on to Kalamazoo, where we were staying. Having arrived in Michigan, we spent a relaxing day with our hosts, and were able to initially enjoy the novelty of the deep snow-covered surroundings.

In the evening we headed off to visit some bikers who were meeting for a social event. The temperatures were well below zero as we climbed into a massive four-by-four. The snow was deep, but these vehicles are more than capable of negotiating the worst of conditions. What they are not so capable of is negotiating sheets of ice, as we were about to discover. We had peeled off the freeway and were now heading down some treacherous back roads. The vehicle was holding its own, with only the slightest sideways slip as the engine powered along these deep snowdrifts. However, we came to a sharp turn in the road, straight onto a long patch of black ice. As the vehicle turned, the ice carried it diagonally across the road and onto the other side. The road was inclining slightly, which meant that traction was virtually impossible, and we were now in a precarious position, sitting on the wrong side of the road. We were sitting ducks for any unsuspecting vehicle that may have been coming the opposite way. Realising this, our driver hit the gas with everything he had, and the wheels spun with unimaginable abandonment. The vehicle then began to edge sideways millimetres at a time. If a truck had been coming the other way, we would have been disintegrated by its force, as there would be no stopping on this sloping ice rink.

We continued to edge back towards our own side of the road as the headlights of a vehicle suddenly came into sight, making its way over the brow of a distant hill. We were still on the wrong side, with wheels now spinning madly. As the vehicle came closer, we realised this was the worst-case scenario. It was actually a large snow plough, with limited visibility as it threw up copious amounts of powdered snow. The plough's wheels made contact with the ice, and there was no stopping it as the truck careered down this frozen slope towards us. With one last push, the four-by-four edged across the imaginary centre line, swinging sideways on its suspension like a pendulum as the force of the air from this great metal snow plough buffeted its sides. Now on the correct side of the road, there appeared to be a little more traction, which allowed us to climb steadily up this death trap. We reached the top of the slope and pulled over, with the realisation of just how close we had been to meeting our Maker. We were all visibly shaken by this experience, and this in an almost bulletproof vehicle.

I do wonder sometimes if we ourselves feel bulletproof, negotiating potentially disastrous situations with abandonment, pretending that we have complete control of our lives. Sure, we have the steering wheel, but we never fully know when conditions may change, when the road ahead may become unstable, when we may lose traction. Those unexpected situations take us by surprise, causing us to lose our grip on the situation as we hit the metaphorical ice and are unable to move. Sometimes, these crisis situations can be an opportunity to reassess our lives, to review the strength of our relationship with God, to allow Him to guide us back onto secure ground.

In that vehicle, we had no real control, no way to steer. If we had continued to be unable to move, we would have been disintegrated by this great metal force. And even when we were able to move, we still lacked any control. Though I have no firm evidence, I personally believe that God had His hand on our lives in that vehicle, preserving us as we inched incrementally back to safety.

We continued on to the club and spent some time chatting and enjoying an American ale or two. We didn't have too much time, however, as I was due to preach at a local church the next morning. Because the snow was so severe, we decided to stay in a hotel overnight, to make sure we actually made it to the church in question, and so we had a comfortable night, though with memories of that near disaster remaining in our minds.

The next morning, we climbed back into the four-by-four and headed off through the snow to the church in Battle Creek, where I was booked to speak. We were a little early, and so the guys decided to wait in the car while I went in and got myself prepared. I entered the church and was greeted by a couple of people who were just preparing the church for a guest. I told them that I was visiting from England and they asked me a few general questions, like did I know the Queen!

I asked them if the pastor was around, and they told me that he was away on this particular morning. This did somewhat surprise me, as the pastor had assured me that he would be there, and I had been looking forward to meeting him. They told me that there was a visiting speaker who was very popular, though. I decided to play along, so I asked if they were any good.

They confirmed that the speaker was a very capable preacher but had never spoken at this particular church before. I thought, 'Yes, I know they haven't!' but it was great that they were so enthusiastic about me speaking there. I asked if there was any coffee available, to which they told me that they had coffee after the service, but they could get me a cup as an exception, as I was visiting from England.

As of yet I hadn't let on that I would be preaching there on this particular morning, and so, as I drank my coffee, I thought I had better let them know that it was me they had been expecting. However, before I had the chance, the two guys who had been waiting in the car came in and beckoned me outside. They informed me that they had made a mistake and we were at the wrong church, ours being at the bottom of the road!

As I climbed into the vehicle, I realised what it must have looked like to those people in the church. I had walked in wearing my leathers, asked about the pastor and questioned them on a visiting speaker, then requested a coffee, without telling them why I had come in or what I wanted with the pastor. I had then put down my coffee and left. I can just imagine the conversations that went on after that service about the mysterious biker who gatecrashed the church, drank their coffee, then left abruptly without a word.

This case of mistaken identity reminded me of a visit to a local pub in Manchester. I had been in touch with an old friend, who told me that this particular pub was where he regularly spent his time, and that he would often pop in at lunchtimes. I had just been visiting my old area and decided to see if I could catch up with him. I had parked my bike outside the window and dropped into this particular pub which, I remembered from my youth, used to have a scattering of sawdust on the floor, with fairly regular bar fights going on.

As I walked in, I asked a few people if they had seen my friend. One of them informed me that he wasn't coming in this particular afternoon, asking me if he was in trouble and if I was after him. He had assumed I was looking for him in order to sort him out for some reason. I could see why he may have thought that, as I had parked the Harley outside and walked through the door dressed in my bike gear. He didn't know who I was, or what my intentions were. After explaining why I was looking for him, the atmosphere became a lot lighter, and he told me he would let my friend know I had been there. With this in mind, I could imagine the two people in church having similar thoughts as I walked in asking for the pastor with no word of explanation. I wouldn't be surprised if they are still wondering what was going on.

It is easy to be misidentified, as with my visit to the church, leaving people to make all manner of judgement calls on who we really are, or our real intentions. In some respects, Jesus was a little like this. He often allowed people to make their own judgement calls on His intentions, on His identity, on His motives. He didn't always correct them immediately either, but allowed people to figure it out for themselves by observing His actions and what He taught. Some, like the religious leaders, assumed He was out to get them, when in reality He wanted to show them a better, more gracious way. Others believed He was a radical, the friend of outcasts, mixing with the unrespectable, someone not to be trusted. He was indeed a radical and a friend of the outcasts, but He was more than that; He was divine, identifiable by miracles and what He taught. If those folk in the pub in Manchester had looked a bit closer, they would have observed the deep red cross sewn on the back of my leather cut-off. The signs that pointed to Jesus' true identity were just as clear, and they would have been obvious if people had dug a little deeper.

Ironically, it was those outcasts who often took the time to dig deeper, and those same outcasts who Jesus opened up to. Thankfully for me, there were people who knew exactly who I was in the next church but had been wondering where I had got to. So, having attended the wrong church, we were now heading off to find the right one. Once we had arrived at the church that had actually been expecting me, I greeted the pastor and related the story, apologising for running a little late. I also told the congregation that this was the second church I had attended that morning. The service went well and it was great chatting to the pastor over a cup of coffee afterwards, which was provided this time by people who actually knew my identity!

This same week, we were due to visit another church in Kalamazoo, where I developed an unexplainable thirst. On the way we had stopped off at a small petrol station in order to pick up a couple of well-needed coffees. Feeling a little hungry, and browsing the aisles, I had come across a rare American delicacy, in the form of beef jerky. What was more, this delicacy had been reduced in price, so I had bought myself a couple of bags. I had carefully opened the packet, removed the flavouring pouch and sprinkled the flavouring onto the cured beef. I couldn't in all honesty taste any difference, after adding the flavouring from the pouch, from that of a normal packet of unflavoured beef jerky.

Two packets later, we arrived at the deep snow-covered car park of the church, and I was feeling particularly parched.

We entered the building, and I was relieved to find that they had Wi-Fi, and more importantly that they were serving coffee. I rang Alison, who was back in Leicester, to see how she was, letting her know where we were and mentioning the beef jerky. Surprisingly, she had never come across beef jerky that contained flavouring, and questioned me on this, recommending I check the packet. Just to prove her wrong, I pulled the empty bag out of my pocket and examined the unmarked packet that had contained the clear crystal flakes. She knew exactly what these were, and let me know that I had probably poisoned myself with silicon crystals, which were there to prevent moisture entering the food. Thankfully, I survived the poisoning, and this explained the reason for my unusual thirst.

Several drinks later, we enjoyed the early morning service, having chatted to some interesting characters. On the way out, though, car tyres were spinning right across the car park, as the snow had worsened. We were fortunate to have travelled in a large four-by-four vehicle, and so we spent the next fifteen minutes pulling cars out of the snow, to where they were able to regain some traction. This had turned into a chaotic scene, with various cars swerving around like salmon caught in a current.

As we were towing the last car out of the snow, a deer suddenly appeared and walked slowly and silently behind the church building in the snow, bringing an unexpected sense of peace and serenity as it moved softly through the trees. For me, in the turmoil that was happening in that car park, this deer felt like a sign that God was present, as a calming influence in the chaos. After the stress of being caught on the ice a couple of days earlier, after nearly poisoning myself with silicon crystals, and now watching these vehicles careering around the car park, this elegant creature cut right through all of it, bringing a real sense of peace. This was certainly what I needed at that moment. I was still more than a little anxious, with the poison moving around my intestines, but this small sign, which I believe was a brief gift from God at that time, certainly helped.

Part Five
On the Road in Europe

18
Prepared to Take the Journey

It was a cold Friday afternoon in early 2009, and I was preparing for the first of many rides into Germany. At the time, I was working as a teacher within a mainstream school in Grantham, Lincolnshire, and the lesson was just about to finish. As the school bell rang, I quickly dismissed the class before stepping into my classroom storage cupboard. I emerged in a manner reminiscent of the old children's show character, Mr Benn, now wearing my leather bike gear, and quickly headed for the bike. I climbed on the Harley, making a swift departure in order to catch the Dover ferry.

As I exited the car park, I immediately hit the Friday rush hour traffic, along with the school pick-up runs, which seemed to be taken in large four-by-four vehicles. I managed to filter along the heavy lanes of slow-moving traffic, which was common in Grantham at that time of the day. I then headed along the busy roads leading to Cambridge and on to Dover, where the ferry would be waiting. I was fairly ill-prepared for this trip, wearing a leather jacket with perforations down the two sides which allowed the cold wind to penetrate straight through. I had also removed the inner lining, which I had placed in a bag, and now the lining had disappeared somewhere along the motorway on the way to the ferry as the wind had lifted it into the air.

I caught the ferry in plenty of time and relaxed for the short journey across the Channel. On disembarking, the weather was reasonably warm, and I headed through France, cut through Belgium and finally into Germany.

I would be riding for at least thirteen hours, and as the day began to draw to a close, the temperature began to drop. The jacket was close-fitting, but I had a woollen jumper in my bag, so I made a couple of stops on the way just to get warm and to put on a few more layers, including the jumper, which provided some insulation, but it was a freezing ride through Germany that evening. As I rode through the Black Forest, I watched the sun going down, and now it was reappearing in the early hours of the morning as I approached Hockenheim. The view almost made up for the freezing environment, as the sun slowly began to light up the tops of the trees, appearing on the horizon in the distance. It was a great experience, having been riding through the depressive, darkened forest, to now see it gradually transformed into a different world, full of life and beauty. There was also a gradual warmth with the coming of the sun, which impacted the freezing sensation that I had experienced.

This reminded me of the imagery from Malachi, when he writes, 'But for you who revere my name, the sun of righteousness will rise with healing in its rays' (Malachi 4:2) – this solar imagery of God's healing presence emerging from the darkness, penetrating and transforming the world, bringing healing where there once was pain. This was very apt and reminded me of the transformed landscape, and not only the physical surroundings, but also the sensation of these healing rays emerging with the sun.

This imagery also comes in the New Testament, where we are given this image of light dawning, transforming lives, bringing life. That life, according to John, was none other than Jesus, who is 'the light of the world' (John 8:12).[27] This was my own story of seeing and experiencing the world differently after a life-changing encounter with God. Now I was riding through

---

[27] See also John 1:1-9.

these transformed surroundings as the sun continued to rise, not fully realised, but holding the promise of a new day.

I had actually been travelling through Germany to meet up with German God's Squad members. At this point, it was not long after recognising a calling to a ministry with bikers, so this trip would be important. Now, thirteen hours later, at four in the morning, I had finally arrived at the house where we were meeting.

The rest of the men were still sleeping, having arrived hours earlier. They reminded me of a colony of seals I had seen in Llandudno, as they lay scattered across the floor, producing various noises that would not be out of place in that same colony. The lady who had answered the door, looking extremely bemused and half-asleep, just pointed to a vacant space on the floor, where I placed my sleeping bag.

I managed to sleep for the next couple of hours, before being woken up again to help get the coffee on for the members of the chapter. These expressions of servanthood are important in the early stages leading to membership, and this was modelled first by Christ to His own disciples, even to the extent of washing their feet.[28]

We enjoyed a much-needed coffee and had something to eat in the garden before climbing on our bikes and heading off to meet with other bikers in the afternoon.

We spent the evening with these bikers, getting to know each other while sharing a few beers. One of the guys, who I was chatting to about faith, invited me to go for a burger at the local fast-food joint across the road in order to talk properly. We sat down, and he offered to get the burgers in. He asked me how many burgers I wanted, which I thought was a strange question. I jokingly replied, 'I couldn't eat more than ten!', not dreaming he would actually order that many.

To my horror, he returned with twenty burgers, ten each, and I wasn't looking forward to the prospect of eating all of

---

[28] John 21:9-12; Matthew 20:28; John 13:1-16.

these, even though they were slightly smaller in size than usual. Having asked for ten burgers, even in jest, I couldn't turn them down; we certainly need to be careful what we wish for! This at least gave us a real chance to chat, if it did also cause my intestines more than a little distress. He shared a little of his life, pointing to a couple of scars which told stories of his life. Interestingly enough, he noticed my own scars which I carry on my right hand, and which also tell their own story of a distant past. In some respects, our scars can be as significant as the tattoos many bikers carry, often holding deep meaning.

For Jesus, too, the physical scars He received hold great significance, as they continue to tell a story of self-sacrifice and love for us. When Thomas looked for evidence of the resurrection, it was the nail marks in Jesus' hands that persuaded him.[29] The scars Jesus carries tell their own story of the crucifixion, of the pain He went through, and of the consequences for us in offering salvation, peace, reconciliation and healing.

Many of us also carry emotional scars, which cannot be seen but are just as real. In some respects, these emotional scars can take a lot longer to heal, which I know from experience, but this is also the transformational nature of faith, where if we allow Him, Jesus can bring healing, even to the deepest emotional wounds that many of us secretly carry.

After discussing some of these physical and emotional scars, I found out later that my companion had been thinking about faith, and I was glad I was able to share a little of my own story.

Having made real inroads with those burgers, we carried the majority of them back to the clubhouse for anyone who wanted one. It was a late night, and I was eventually relieved just to shut my eyes for a while on a nearby seat, now feeling exhausted from serious sleep deprivation.

The trip was certainly worthwhile, but this was one of those thankfully rare examples where I needed to function with little

---

[29] John 20:27-29.

sleep, not to mention the hours of gruelling miles in the saddle. It is interesting, however, the way God works, drawing us into conversations we couldn't imagine having, or situations we might never have considered if we hadn't been prepared to take the journey. But we need to be ready for these opportunities, because we never know the impact they may have on someone's life for the better.

19

Travelling Mercies

In June 2015, I was travelling to visit some members of God's Squad in Holland. However, this was also an important ride for me for other reasons. My son Luke, who lives in Glasgow, had invited me to the first night of his stag weekend in Belgium. I was going to stop off on the way back from Holland, in order to attend.

I had packed everything I needed for this trip, as well as all the documentation, or so I believed. I was heading for the ferry in Dover, and this was the time when the Calais Border Force was clamping down heavily. When I travel alone, I tend to do the journey in one go, stopping only in Dover to fill up with petrol before I board the ferry. I was running slightly late, so I was in a rush as Alison handed me my passport, which I then placed in my jacket pocket. I was now on my way, moving rapidly towards the ferry. The roads were relatively free of traffic and the journey was quicker than I had anticipated. I stopped briefly to fill up at Dover, at my usual petrol station, and headed across the roundabout and into the ferry terminal.

I pulled up with plenty of time to spare and collected my paper ticket. I handed over my passport, and the woman took it off me, disappearing back into the booth. She looked at the passport, then looked at me, then looked back at the passport, a little puzzled. She asked me to take off my sunglasses, which was usual. There were all sorts of scenarios running through my head. Had I been caught speeding, or failed to stop at the search area on the way in, or had my back patch caused concern? I soon found out, as she looked me straight in the eyes, saying, 'You have changed a bit, haven't you!'

I said, 'Yes I do look a little different.'

I then began to wrack my brains to remember how I might know her; did I know her from school, did we work together in the past? She handed back my passport, pointing to the picture. It was the likeness of a woman with long hair and blue eyes. In fact, it was a spitting image of my wife.

In my rush to leave, Alison had handed me her passport. I explained to the woman at security what had happened, and she walked over to her colleague and asked him a few questions. I could imagine being prosecuted for fraud at this point. She returned to me and asked me for further identification, and I showed her my driving licence. She told me that I would be able to cross using my driving licence on this occasion, as my wife's last name was the same as mine on my licence. However, she told me that the border force in Calais were being very difficult at the moment, and it was doubtful that they would let me through at their end or, worse still, allow me to return. She was actually smiling and obviously found the whole affair extremely amusing, but I was just glad to have someone supportive to help me.

I then phoned my wife to let her know what was happening, but she had worked it out just after I had left. She was now more than halfway to Dover, having got her mother to drive her, so that she could give me my own passport, but she was stuck in heavy traffic. There were also problems with the ferries, and I wasn't guaranteed to get on another one that day. I decided to risk it and, much to my mother-in-law's frustration, they then drove back to Leicester without even visiting Dover.

I was permitted to board the ferry and had an anxious journey into Calais. On arrival, however, there was no sign of any extra security, or even the extra staff that had been predicted. I rode down the ramp and straight out of the terminal without being required to stop at any point.

I completed my trip and stopped off at Belgium on the way back as planned. I parked outside the hotel, where Luke's friends were sitting drinking Belgian beer, which they bought me a pint of. We had a good night, which was obviously more sedate than it would be once I had departed the next morning. My other son, Benjamin, living in Leicester, had brought my passport over for me, which made life a lot easier.

This whole scenario makes me consider the way Jesus travelled on a different passport. This was actually God, the Creator, the one who dwelt in heaven, who had entered our world, who had become a man, who became like us. His true nature was not recognised as He taught, healed and performed miracles. Jesus was travelling on a human passport, as He humbled himself, as He brought forgiveness. Jesus' true likeness was also on a different passport, a likeness of God the Father. But for Jesus, He didn't just travel as a man, He became a man, while He also didn't stop being God; He remained both, human and divine. In some respect Jesus had dual nationality.[30]

As Jesus walked along the Emmaus Road[31] after His resurrection, His disciples didn't fully recognise Him; there was something different. Once their eyes had been opened, they recognised Him as the person they had spent so long with, but at the same time there was also something of His divinity revealed. From a case of mistaken identity, Jesus' true nature was eventually recognised. His dual citizenship of both earth and heaven was finally seen, and remains so.

At the start of 2018, I was preparing to ride back over to Holland. This would be a fast ride as I only had two days to complete the trip, needing to be back on Sunday morning for church. I had packed the day before, in order to reach the Dover ferry in plenty of time. I was travelling for a significant meeting, which I knew would hold several challenges.

---

[30] Philippians 2:6-11.

[31] Luke 24:13-35.

It was a fairly straightforward ride, with no real hiccups on the way. The ferry was on time, and I had the opportunity to take a steady ride through France and into Holland. What is helpful on these long rides is the opportunity to pray, especially when heading into what can be unpredictable situations.

As I continued to pray, I entered a long stretch of Dutch highway containing three lanes. I was sitting in the middle lane, having just overtaken a car, and I was suddenly joined by a solitary goose, which revealed an enormous wingspan. The goose pulled up right next to the bike in the right-hand lane, and began to fly parallel to me. The goose matched my speed, and I could almost have put my hand out to touch it as it flew in line with my shoulders. With its enormous wingspan, it actually filled the inside lane as it claimed its spot on the motorway. As I looked back, there was a queue of cars driving steadily and patiently behind this goose. I thought it would just fly off, but it remained next to me for the next fifteen minutes or so, as we moved steadily along the lane. I eventually accelerated, leaving the goose behind, where it then flew back into the fields from which it had appeared.

I related this to my host, who said, 'That sounds like a description of the Holy Spirit.' In fact, in the Celtic Christian tradition, the Holy Spirit was always symbolised by a wild goose, rather than a dove. This image resonated with me, and I do believe that this was God's way of telling me that His Holy Spirit would be at my side, bringing peace and wisdom into a difficult situation, and this I subsequently experienced during the discussions of the weekend. This image will stay with me for life, along with the imagery of God's Holy Spirit, who travels with us as we ride.

I had taken several rides to Switzerland over the years, and was eager to return. It was now June 2018, and several months on from the recent ride to Holland, as well as one week before my ordination within the Church of England. Nevertheless, I had decided that it would be a good idea to embark on another round trip to Switzerland on the Harley. I had arranged to stay with the Swiss God's Squad chapter, which would be a great opportunity to share fellowship together. I decided to take a leisurely ride, taking in some scenery on the way, and had therefore decided to travel to Switzerland alone.

I travelled light, ensuring to pack one of the most essential items in my bag: a European adapter plug. This was essential in order to charge my mobile phone and to power the portable kettle I often carry, so I could make tea or coffee in the mornings. I felt confident and secure that I had everything packed, knowing I was prepared for any contingency on this ride.

I had decided to ride through France initially, and on disembarking from the ferry I headed swiftly for St Quentin. I spent the night in the usual low-budget motel, utilising the essential kettle to make a flask of coffee, and headed off.

I had decided to take in some of the sights in Strasbourg, which is a picturesque old town with a famous cathedral. On the evening on which I had decided to stop over, there was a famous light show being projected onto the whole length of one side of the cathedral. This was spectacular, and was accompanied by well-chosen classical music. One particular section of this show revealed an ominous face appearing in one of the cathedral's windows, followed by a shadowy figure climbing out and crawling along the length of the cathedral and onto its roof. This show was mesmerising, as the atmospheric music accompanied the movements in this skilfully choreographed performance.

I returned to my room and went to plug in my phone, also intending to make an evening mug of coffee. To my horror, I came to the realisation that I had left my power adapter and charger in the motel room at St Quentin. This now meant that I couldn't use my kettle, which was bad enough, but more importantly I was unable to charge my phone. Furthermore, without my phone, I had no way of contacting my host, having only a vague idea where I was due to be staying the following evening.

I spent the next morning in Strasbourg frantically searching for a phone charger which, after several hours, I eventually managed to purchase, with the intention of charging my phone in a motorway service station en route to Switzerland. However, arriving at the border without passing any service stations, and out of pure desperation, I rode back into France, where I entered a French coffee shop. This was a good move, as I now realised too that I hadn't exchanged any Swiss currency. Using all the charm I could muster, along with my extensive French language skills, which consisted of *'Bonjour, madame'*, I asked the waitress if I could use a socket to charge my phone for ten minutes while I drank my coffee. This gave me a couple of minutes emergency air time.

As I crossed the Swiss border, I felt like the disciples who had been sent out by Jesus, not knowing where they were going to stay, being at the mercy of strangers, with no food and no money.[32] I did manage to find a service station in Switzerland, where I bought another coffee and went to plug the charger in. It was at this point that I realised the charger did not actually fit the Swiss power outlets, which made it obsolete. It was feeling like a disaster of a trip, and I should have considered the Lord's words to Paul: 'My grace is sufficient for you, for my power is made perfect in weakness' (2 Corinthians 12:9).

As I headed for Geneva, I briefly started my phone up, making use of the little charge I had gained in the French café, and was able to receive a brief signal. My phone worked just long enough to read a text that had been sent by one of the God's Squad members I would be staying with, along with a postcode, which I inputted quickly into the sat nav.

On arrival, I found that if I had taken money on this particular occasion, I wouldn't have been able to spend it, as the Swiss chapter I was visiting insisted on buying food, beer and, more importantly, coffee. I was given a European adapter, and their generosity was incredibly humbling. We had opportunity

---

[32] Luke 9:1-6.

to pray together, to encourage each other and to get to know one another better. From a position of weakness and vulnerability, I experienced God's grace. I also experienced God's grace working through Christians I had never met before, and I was blessed by their generosity and love.

We all have times when we feel fairly helpless, when we realise we can't do things in our own strength. The apostle Paul experienced so many times like this on his own journeys, and related how he had been placed in prison, flogged, shipwrecked, been hungry, 'cold and naked', in 2 Corinthians 11:23-28. We all have our own stories, but these are the times when we again need to remember that Jesus strengthens us when we are weak through His grace, which was certainly my experience on this particular trip.

20
Travels in the Pandemic

In the summer of 2020, I had the opportunity to ride over to Prague. I was actually visiting this ancient city on a return journey from Poland, during the two weeks when we had been permitted to travel during the COVID-19 pandemic.

Prague was a beautiful city, and as I rode along its ancient streets, the lack of traffic was both noticeable and refreshing. Ordinarily, this city teems with people and remains a popular tourist destination, but now, during the pandemic, there were very few tourists around. I made my way to its historic centre and found a wonderful, ancient, wooden hotel, overlooking the famous historic Charles Bridge, which spanned the scenic and picturesque Vltava River. I parked the bike and settled into this magnificent building, taking in the panoramic views of the town. I then strolled steadily over an almost desolate bridge, which is ordinarily covered with sightseers moving across it like ants streaming along a branch. I wandered past the various street artists, trinket stalls and jewellery tables that had been set up in an *ad hoc* manner. Having crossed the bridge, I wandered past the unique architectural monuments, looking up at a famous astrological clock with moving wooden figures, large interwoven cogs, loud chimes and ancient music emanating from it.

I then took in the more peaceful scenery, the ancient churches and other intricate bridges, while listening to classical music through my earphones, which was fitting for such a magnificent city. In that moment, without the usual stag parties and crowds of sightseers, there was a real sense of God's presence.

There was one particular piece of music by Karl Jenkins that particularly resonated with my soul as I wandered the city, set to the ancient lyrics of 'Ave Verum Corpus'. The beauty of the song and its ability to touch the soul compelled me to look for the interpretation of the actual words. I discovered that the words are Eucharistic by nature, going back centuries, and in essence remind us of Jesus' miraculous birth, of His sacrificial death on the cross, of His suffering and our future hope.[33]

It struck me that God speaks and inspires in the most unexpected ways, and for me during those four days spent in Prague – which were spent fairly consistently listening to classical music – this was certainly an unexpected experience, as I had never been absorbed by this music genre before.

Having taken in this amazing ancient city with its spectacular culture, I had now experienced the highs of the city. However, on the last day, I wandered past the picturesque scenes towards an old city square. It was here that I came across a small group of homeless men. I bought some food to share with the three men who were sitting on a long wooden bench, and chatted for a while. As I sat talking with them, my eyes were drawn to the leg of one of the men, whose trouser leg had ridden up, exposing a deep festering sore. As I looked closer, his leg was actually rotting from the inside, reminiscent of a tree trunk with a long deep split along the grain, being devoured by woodlice.

The man sat staring into space with dead eyes while flies landed on this festering sore, moving deep into his rotting flesh, almost unnoticed by the man himself. I asked his friend why he hadn't been taken to a hospital. He told me that he couldn't afford to go, and that no one cared about an old man on the streets in this city. He repeated, with pain in his eyes, 'It's a

---

[33] www.classicfm.com/discover-music/ave-verum-corpus-lyrics (accessed 13th October 2023).

tragedy, it's a tragedy.' I looked for a chemist but was unable to find one, and in reality there was little I could do for him in the half-hour I had left in this city.

I left with immense sadness in my heart, and this man's leg has imprinted itself on my memory. It felt sad to see the beauty of this great city, when at its centre there was so much pain. I was heartbroken and filled with a real sense of remorse and guilt at being unable to help, and as I rode to meet my travelling companion who was waiting for me, and who would be accompanying me to Germany, I couldn't shake the sadness in the man's eyes. My only sense of hope came from knowing that Jesus came for such as these and knows their hearts, and these men were in my prayers. The piece of music that had resonated so much as I wandered the city now took on a more pertinent significance in the midst of this great human 'tragedy'.

On leaving Prague, it was a short ride through the Czech Republic into Germany, where we had decided to visit the home of a German God's Squad member. The journey took longer than we anticipated, as the throttle cable on my Dutch companion's Harley snapped as we travelled down the German highway. He managed to ride the bike to the nearest service station by gripping the inner wire of the throttle cable in order to keep the bike moving. I spent the next hour helping him to remove the secondary wire from his throttle, and to reroute it, so that the throttle now needed to be rotated in the opposite direction, which also required some coordination from my companion.

We finally arrived at the home where we had arranged to stop the night, later than anticipated. It was good, though, to then be able to share fellowship together over a couple of local German lagers, chatting about our experiences on the road.

The following morning our German brother accompanied us to a mechanic friend of his, who fitted new cables to the throttle of the Harley. We then had lunch together before heading off once more onto the highway.

Having departed from Germany and put some serious miles behind us, we were now well on our way to Holland where we would part company and I would catch my ferry to England. As this was in the middle of lockdown, travel was a continual problem and things were still in flux. I had booked a cheap hotel in Holland as my ferry was not due to leave until the following morning, so I had plenty of time, or so I thought. What I didn't know was that the UK government had decided to bring in a two-week quarantine period for anyone entering the country, and had decided that the cut-off time would be four o'clock in the morning. This meant that my ferry would not make it on time and I would need to self-isolate for two weeks, which I certainly couldn't afford to do. In the meantime, I was blissfully unaware of this as we rode steadily towards Holland, making what appeared to be good progress.

We pulled into a service station to fill up and buy a coffee. As we sat and drank our coffee, I gave Alison a ring, and it was at this point that she informed me of the inevitability that I would need to quarantine when I returned. The ferry companies had put on a couple of additional ferries, but these had been booked up immediately. The situation appeared hopeless, as all options for getting to England before 4am were now exhausted.

We returned to our bikes and set of for the final leg of the journey, fuelled up and now not needing to stop before we arrived. In the meantime, my wife had located one final ferry leaving from Calais that would get me home before the cut-off point, but this would mean diverting immediately towards France and riding through the night in order to board at 1am. The problem was that we were now unable to receive calls, and I had no idea this was a possibility. One thing I did do, however, as we rode this final leg, was to pray that God would find a way to get me back on time, but with little faith.

We were now close to Utrecht, where I felt a compulsion to pull into a service station, with no obvious reason to do so, as we had more than enough fuel, but there was an inner compulsion prompting me. As we dismounted from our bikes, the reason became clear, as Alison had at that same moment felt prompted by God to phone me one last time to let me know that she had found the last ferry to depart, and that she would book me on board. If she hadn't phoned at that exact point when we had stopped, it would have been too late to divert to France in time, and it was already cutting it fine. God's timing, however, is perfect!

The next few hours were tense, as I was forced to divert through Belgium in order to reach the ferry in time. However, Belgium had now closed its borders to UK citizens owing to the pandemic. I had no choice, though, and moved with trepidation across the border, with not a little anxiety at every Belgian police car that came into sight. The relief was tangible as I finally crossed Belgium's border into France on this final, exhausting journey leading into the early hours of the morning, and onwards to Calais. I had been riding quicker than I had liked, and only just made the ferry before it departed, but I was at last on board. What could possibly go wrong now?!

Having ridden for sixteen hours without sleep, I was exhausted. I managed to sleep for an hour as the ferry travelled steadily towards Dover. The ferry finally came into port, and I made my way to the bike. However, as I started the engine and pulled in the clutch cable in order to kick the bike into gear, there was no reaction. To my horror, I realised that somewhere between parking the bike and climbing back on, the clutch cable had snapped. Without a clutch, it was impossible to change gear, and unless the bike is in neutral there is no way to start it, but I needed to get it off the ferry. The only hope was to get a push down the slope of the ferry, kick it into gear while at the same time starting the engine. I then needed to make sure I didn't have to stop, especially at the checkpoints leaving the ferry port. Fortunately, in the early hours of the morning there were no security staff around. I was then able to ride out of the port, cross the roundabout and head onto the motorway. Because I was riding through the early hours, this meant that the usual traffic jams had dispersed, and I was able to keep on riding without the need to stop. I thought nothing could hinder me from now getting home to some desperately needed sleep.

As I headed for the motorway, I looked down at the fuel gauge, only to discover that the tank was empty. In the rush to reach the ferry, I hadn't had the chance to fill up in Calais, where my tank had moved well below the reserve point. The problem now was that I couldn't stop at any local petrol stations, because I wouldn't be able to get the bike going again owing to the snapped clutch cable. The only way I could fill up was by stopping at a motorway service station with a ramp, in order to glide back down and kick it into gear again. It was thirty miles to the motorway petrol station, and the tank was now completely empty. I was literally riding on fumes, and it was doubtful it would hit three miles, never mind thirty. I figured I would continue until the bike stopped and then glide onto the hard shoulder. However, I also thought it may be worth praying that God would get me to the service station against all the odds, but I didn't in all honesty have much faith.

I glanced back at the fuel dial, which had just hit empty, and it now moved halfway into the reserve point on the dial! I couldn't believe what I was seeing. Furthermore, the gauge remained there for the next thirty miles, without fluctuation, until I reached the service station, at which point it fell back to where it had been thirty miles back, totally empty.

This trip had certainly increased my faith, as I had experienced God's providence in a quantifiable way.

There are several accounts in the Bible where God did similar things, such as the account of Elijah and a widow in 1 Kings 17:7-16 Here, Elijah the prophet asked a widow for some bread to eat, but the widow only had a very small quantity of oil in a jug, as well as a little flour. God told Elijah that until the rains came, neither the oil or the flour would run out. So Elijah, the widow and her son were able to eat bread made by this endless supply of oil and flour, until it was again available. This was certainly my experience of the petrol in the tank which didn't run out until I no longer needed it and was able to fill the tank once more.

For some people, this will be difficult to believe, but I know how far the remaining petrol in that tank would have taken me, and I know that it was naturally impossible to travel as far as I did. But that was the reality, and having seen this for myself, I cannot doubt the way God is able to respond to our prayers in times of desperation, as with Elijah.

21

Provision

In August of 2022, I returned to Switzerland, heading again through France and Germany to get to Geneva. This trip would also give me the opportunity to ride fairly extensively through the Swiss Alps, which is not always possible on shorter trips.

On this occasion the engine ran like a dream, and my tyres remained inflated in all the important places. I was again staying with members of God's Squad, where I would have the opportunity to share fellowship and ride with some of the other members of the chapter. Again, the scenery was spectacular as I rode with the other members down to Lake Geneva, which lies beneath a set of winding tracks leading down from the house where I was staying. We followed the track which wound through the vineyards, heavy with grapes, before glimpsing the crystal blue waters of Lake Geneva, which absolutely took my breath away.

The following day, however, on waking up, I noticed that the rear tyre had lost air and was fairly soft. I decided to inflate it and see how it fared both the next day and overnight. The tyre appeared to remain inflated, and it looked like all was well.

On the final day, I decided to spend the morning riding across the Alps with another chapter member. We followed a valley that led through some more magnificent scenery, winding through undulating fields and leading to a local beauty spot. Here, we had lunch overlooking a lake in this long, flowing valley. We then returned across the top of the Alps, with equally magnificent views. We ended with a descent, which wound sharply and steeply down another breathtaking mountain pass. This was one of the most amazing rides you could take, owing both to the bird's-eye views of the valley below and to the perfect bends which allowed the bike to lean deep into the corners as the road flowed steadily downwards. The bike, however, appeared to be sluggish, and was a little heavy on the steering as it accelerated round these sharp bends. I thought little of it, though, and we continued our ride.

We concluded with a steep climb up a single track, hemmed in by a wire fence on either side to keep the cows from straying. The track consisted of dirt and gravel, and ended with an extremely steep climb without barriers, leading to a lodge overlooking the hillside. This place was very special, and I wouldn't have missed sitting overlooking those views, drinking coffee with a good friend, for the world. However, if I had realised what had been making the bike so heavy through the corners, as the tyre had begun to gradually lose air, I may not have been so keen to have ridden those sheer, single-track inclines that day.

Having ridden some challenging tracks in the morning, I decided to ride into town on the final afternoon of the trip. Here, while visiting a Harley Davidson shop, my tyre went completely flat. As I began to ride away, I realised this, and pushed the bike back into its parking space with a little help from a biker who had been standing outside when I arrived. I had little option than to get the mechanic at the Harley dealer to change the inner tube. I was reluctant to do this for two reasons. First, I don't like anyone else working on my bike, as I maintain it myself, and second, the cost of repairs here was higher than I would have normally been prepared to pay. However, I believe God had already provided for this contingency a few days prior to visiting the shop. After riding with some of the Swiss God's Squad members along the Alps a few days previously, one of them had come up to me and handed me an envelope. He had said, 'God has told me to give this to you, as you will need it.'

When I opened the envelope there was a sum of money inside, and while I was reluctant to take it, he insisted that God had told him to give this to me, and that I would be needing it. This now made sense, as the cost of the repair was the exact amount he had given me a couple of days before! This convinced me that the whole incident was in God's hands – even finding the flat outside the Harley shop on the last day, where I was able to get it fixed for the start of the 700-mile ride back to England in the morning. If the tyre had gone down a few hours before, on one of those steep single-track inclines, I doubt I would be here to recall any of this.

I could clearly recognise God's protection on that ride – even more, the way God spoke to one of the Swiss guys a few days before about providing the money to repair something that had not yet occurred, with the exact amount!

No sooner had I returned from Switzerland than I was heading back, now in September 2022. This was a short visit, unlike the previous occasion, just a month after returning. This time it was necessary to fly. I was spending the weekend with another Swiss God's Squad member, two Irish singers and a couple of Irish God's Squad members. We were staying with a gracious Swiss family and attending a wedding celebration together.

As we had some free time before the wedding, we had a chance to visit one of Switzerland's country trails around a peaceful and serene lake. These times are really important, just ambling along, chatting together, sharing fellowship. I think Jesus would have probably enjoyed doing the same thing, wandering around the Sea of Galilee with His mates. I can imagine some of His parables coming out of these times, as He noticed the ordinary things around Him that might describe the kingdom of God. I could imagine Him drawing analogies from the lake, the vegetation or even the ordinary people He met on the way, who He could share time with.

We sat out and ate together, while enjoying each other's company, before returning to the house. The legal part of the wedding was held in the village, down a steep, winding lane. We had been fortunate to borrow a couple of Harleys, which we rode to the venue. The only problem was that the Harley Road King which I had borrowed had been fitted out with exceptionally high ape hanger handlebars, which meant my arms were held high up on the grips. This is fine, unless the first time you ride the bike is around tight steep bends, the type we were now negotiating. The ride was interesting, to say the least, as I fought to manoeuvre the bike round the corners to keep up with the leading vehicle, as I didn't know the way, while also watching out for traffic on the other side of the road. The bike was actually extremely comfortable, and once past the tight bends it was a pleasure to ride.

After the preliminaries, we returned briefly to the house to collect various items for the wedding party. We were then back on the bikes and heading for the main part of the wedding ceremony. This took us along beautiful winding lanes, past vivid green fields and along low mountain passes. The wedding celebrations took place next to a ski lift, in a wooden ski café/restaurant, which we had taken over for the wedding. We were surrounded by a herd of cows and several young horses, which for some reason were all wearing bells.

The wedding was incredible, God was clearly present and I had the chance to chat with several bikers about faith. It was also good to be able to chat with some French-speaking Swiss bikers about faith within our club context. The celebration was loud, full of joy, full of love and full of laughter – very loud laughter!

Around 3.30am, those remaining awake, including myself, the Irish guests and a couple of Swiss bikers, started to move towards the row of bunk beds. I climbed on top of a bed and slept well until I was woken up again at 7am to help put tables, chairs, amps and other items away before we rode back to the house.

When everyone had departed, I decided to have a peaceful walk down to the village. It wasn't particularly far away and took around twenty-five minutes to get there. The walk was pleasant, winding along scenic streets, then following a row of steps down towards the base of the mountain. As I arrived in the village, I passed a man drinking, who stopped me and wanted to chat. We talked for a while, and I told him a little of my life and about my trip to Switzerland. He asked me if I wanted to get a drink with him, but I told him that I really needed to get back to catch a plane in a few hours. The next thing I knew, his arms were around me and he was giving me a massive hug, which was actually quite moving.

It had been easy to find my way down the mountainside to the village, but now all roads looked the same. I found myself well and truly lost for the next couple of hours, wandering aimlessly past possible routes back. As with the roads, these numerous steps and walkways were identical. I realised that if I didn't find my way back soon I would miss the flight, but I hadn't put my friend's number in my phone. I eventually managed to get an internet signal and contacted my Swiss biker friend, using social media, to guide me back to the house.

Whether we are at a raucous wedding celebration or walking in the peace of a Swiss village, I believe God can lead us into some fascinating conversations and encounters. He can lead us at times into opportunities to bring some hope to those who are feeling as lost as I had been, wandering around the base of the mountain; sometimes we just need a friend to guide us back.

22
This Little Light

It was a cold January morning in 2022 as I climbed onto the Harley for another long ride. I headed straight off towards the ferry that would take me to Germany, but I hadn't realised just how cold it was going to get. I was riding over to attend the funeral of a good friend who had been a faithful member of God's Squad, where I was due to speak and offer support to the God's Squad members there.

There was a bitter wind cutting into my jacket as I rode down the M1 motorway, passing numerous cars and lorries. I approached the usual bottlenecks and speed restrictions, once more filtering between the morning traffic. One blessing had been that I had just purchased a pair of heated gloves, which were now doing their job well in the midst of this biting wind. I reached the ferry with little time to spare, glad to be boarding a warm environment, where I could sit down for a coffee.

Although I had often done this trip in one go, I had decided to stop off in Lille for some relaxation before continuing the journey. This was where things began to go wrong, as I attempted to follow the satnav, which appeared to be getting confused about its directions. Riding through this typical old French town, the satnav attempted to take me onto a pedestrian area. This felt all wrong as I followed the road round, straight into the path of two French traffic officers sitting on bright yellow sports bikes. I was signalled to pull over and dismount.

Neither of the officers appeared willing to communicate with me in English, as they refused to answer any of my questions. They took a picture of the bike, noted the number plate and asked to see my licence. Although seemingly very reluctant to give me any information, one of them told me that I would receive two heavy fines. The first was owing to me riding down this road which was out of bounds for motorcycles. The second was owing to my exhaust, which they felt was too loud. There was no mechanism for detecting the volume, so the fine appeared a little arbitrary. There really wasn't any point arguing about these fines, and I realised that I had no log book with me, so could have been in more trouble if I had complained.

I carried on along the street, finding St Maurice Church, which sat opposite the hotel, and pulled up next to the main door. It was at this point, still smarting at the harsh fines, that I left my gloves on the saddle while I booked in. I returned to the bike to find this pair of gloves, which I had owned for twenty-four hours, had been stolen. I was then advised not to leave my bike outside the hotel, as the area was a bad one, and I may wake up to find the bike gone. However, I had left the bike in all manner of bad places, and so I told the owner I would risk it.

Once unpacked, I decided to go for a stroll around this historic centre, which was really interesting. I did find myself looking down at everyone's hands, still living in hope that I may find the gloves. I had a great steak for dinner at a local place, with a glass of extremely good French wine. I then wandered back, stopping for a coffee at a street vendor's, where a small crowd of drinkers had gathered. I chatted with them for a while before heading for the hotel.

The next day I decided to have one last look for these gloves, realising that the outside of the church was a place where the homeless guys slept. I decided to check to see if any of these guys had seen the gloves, but to no avail. I finally spoke to one man who had been carrying his length of cardboard – on which he had been sleeping – across the square, in order to stash it out of sight. He had also helped some of the other men tidy up their sleeping areas. He was eager to chat and had a good grasp of English, and asked me if I would like to join him for coffee. What this really meant was, 'Would you like to buy me a coffee?'

He took me to what he described as the best coffee shop in town, and he wasn't wrong. I asked him if he wanted something to eat, but he declined, asking just for coffee. We ambled back, chatting for ten minutes or so as we drank our coffee, and he shared with me that he was actually a Christian himself.

I had been so tied up with my own feelings at the loss of my gloves that I had failed to see the tragedy of these men who surrounded this ancient church. My hands would be cold for a couple of days, while these guys would be freezing for weeks on end. In some respects, this man, who was looking after his fellow homeless neighbours, far from wanting something from me, was offering the hand of friendship in a foreign country, keeping me company on that freezing morning. I had been more than a little fed up at having been fined and at losing my gloves, but I left the town a little ashamed, and was now hoping that these gloves had been taken by someone who really needed them, which was something that my wife said when I phoned her. I feel that God was challenging my attitude here, reminding me that Jesus came with compassion for the poor and destitute – as these guys were.

I left Lille, never to return, and began the long journey to Germany. The initial ride was fairly pleasant, if a little cold, but the road eventually began to climb. My fingertips were now becoming numb, as I had only brought a spare pair of summer gloves, which were not helping at all. I then hit a heavy rain storm, which took the temperature down even further. My boots began to take in water and my toes began to lose their feeling. I was now hitting the tops of the peaks, where snow was lying on the sides of the road and slightly covering the forest surface. I carried on across the peaks, riding through the odd snow-covered stretch, until the road began to head downwards. It was getting dark now, and I needed petrol.

I pulled over at a petrol station, and on stopping dropped the bike, having now lost all feeling in my fingers. I managed to pick it up, but had broken the end of the front brake lever and damaged the right footboard. I didn't at the time realise, though, that a bolt on the footboard had actually sheared off.

Having filled up, and regained some feeling in my fingers, I rode the remainder of the route, almost to where I was staying, until my footboard dislodged and tipped forward. I managed to find a garage that lent me a spanner to tighten up the footboard, but I now couldn't apply any pressure to it. I did somehow eventually make it to the house where I was stopping for the night, and in the morning I managed to scavenge a bolt from one of the rear pegs in order to secure the footboard for the ride home.

Despite the difficulties getting there, it had been important for me to ride over to attend this funeral, and to have been given the privilege of speaking on behalf of the club, as the only non-German voice in the service. It was humbling also to see the number of people's lives that this German Christian brother had touched. He was certainly much loved, and a good witness to his faith and to God. We spent the evening remembering his life and sharing fellowship together, but in the morning I had to leave early in order to make Calais, this time in one hit.

Although there was still the odd spattering of snow, the temperature was not half as cold as it had been on the way. The wife of the God's Squad member whose funeral I had attended gave me a pair of warmer gloves which had belonged to her husband, and which helped with the cold on the ride back. As I rode over the peaks, I could see the stretches of ice, something I was glad I hadn't been aware of on the way.

I had ridden for some hours now, and my petrol tank was getting low. I stopped at a few stations, but one was closed down, one had no petrol and a further one only had a system for paying at the pump that was not actually working. Things were getting desperate, and it would have been disastrous to be stuck on these desolate frozen roads. I began to pray hard as I looked down at the fuel gauge, which was now halfway into reserve, and with no petrol stations registering on the satnav along the way.

Things were looking hopeless as I crossed the brow of a hill, but I noticed a dim light in the distance. I carried on riding on fumes as I approached a turn-off leading to a village on the hill. Taking the unexpected turning and riding a little further, I realised the light I had seen was in fact the lights of this village, complete with a café and a petrol station! This may just have saved me from freezing, and if it hadn't been for the light, I would have ridden right past it.

This reminds me of a parable of Jesus, where He says, 'You are the light of the world. A town built on a hill cannot be hidden' (Matthew 5:14). This was certainly true here as this town was lit up like a beacon. However, Jesus was actually referring to the need for Christians to live with the light of Christ shining before people – letting others see God through the way we live, through our testimony of Jesus as the One who came to bring light into a dark world. It struck me that this was what my friend had done, with so many people having heard about Jesus, and I recognised the way his life had been impacted by Jesus in the way He lived.

The light of Christ is life-giving, just as this light on a hill was to me, as I filled my bike up once more and found sustenance for the journey.

23
God's Appointments

It wasn't a particularly popular decision, especially with Bethany, my daughter, to visit Ukraine in the June of 2022, not many months after the country had been invaded. However, I was travelling to spend time with the chapter of God's Squad in order to encourage them, as well as to carry funds that the church had generously raised and which I now carried in my pocket, in cash! I had arrived in Poland, at Krakow airport, where I would spend the night, before catching a bus that would carry me over the border and into Lviv.

On arriving at the bus station, there was some confusion about my ticket, which had needed to be booked well in advance, and the driver was clearly not going to let me on. He actually spoke little English, but was able to say 'no' fairly well. It didn't seem good, and I was not looking forward to returning to England. However, a man stepped forward and began interceding for me, so that the driver eventually agreed to let me on. If he hadn't been there, I very much doubt that I would have actually made it past Poland.

This has been my experience on many of my trips, where someone has either assisted me or spoken up for me. This was the experience of the early Church, too, where the Holy Spirit often prompted people to help or guide those early Christians, sometimes even through visions.[34] The Holy Spirit is actually

---

[34] Acts 16:7-10.

identified by Jesus as an 'advocate' (John 14:16-17), one who will intercede for us, and I am convinced that the Holy Spirit has been active in many precarious situations along the road.

Having finally managed to board the bus, we were now heading for the Polish border. The bus pulled up at the first border crossing, joining a long queue and falling in line behind several other buses. We were told to hold up our passports, and there was a unified sea of blue, with one solitary red British passport sticking out like a sore thumb. Nevertheless, after several hours, the bus crossed both borders, and I was relieved to actually be in Ukraine and heading for my destination.

One other problem, however, was that my phone didn't work across the border, and I now had no way of contacting the Ukrainians who were going to pick me up; neither did I have a clear idea of where to get off the bus. Fortunately, the Ukrainian lady who sat next to me spoke perfect English, and was able to translate the writing on my ticket; in fact, she was getting off just before me.

Again, although I was travelling alone, I am convinced that God was by my side every step of the way during this whole trip. I am also sure both the interpreter at the bus station and this lady who spoke perfect English had been prompted to help me on this journey in response to my prayers. I know that God often puts people into our paths, and at other times puts us into other people's paths, leading to some interesting conversations.

We eventually arrived at Lviv, and I managed to get off at the right stop. I then found a Wi-Fi link at a train station and was able to contact my hosts. Having been picked up by a member of the chapter, we spent an evening in fellowship with the other members, where we prayed together and read the Bible, and they sang some spiritual songs in their own language.

The following day I was able to borrow a Harley, and I went for a short ride through Lviv with my host. On the surface, it could have been any ordinary day, with people going about their daily lives, until one of the men I was staying with commented, 'We are living like bachelors now.' As I sat with the men, I realised the pain of being separated from family, from wives, from children. In all of this, though, these men were continuing to help feed the dispossessed, and those who were ministers among them were also continuing to give spiritual support to others. Within this ominous atmosphere, where life continued, there was also a constant threat of missiles never far away.

The next day, we headed for Kyiv, stopping off to fill an armoured vehicle with items that were needed for those who had been dispossessed, using the cash I had brought with me. We then drove to drop these items off at a collection centre in a safer area, which one of the men's wives was helping to coordinate, as they were forced to live apart owing to the invasion.

After stopping for the night on the way, we continued the next day in a black four-by-four vehicle to Kyiv. We briefly stopped on the side of the road, where I unwisely wandered onto the verge. I was told that this was where several landmines had been buried, and I could have inadvertently stepped on one.

The city held clues that invasion had been attempted. In fact, on one of the days, we rode our bikes across a bridge to attend a funeral that was on the opposite side of the river, which divides the city into two regions. As we rode across the bridge, I was struck by several long, deep crevices in the road, which would have destroyed the bike if we had hit one. However, on this occasion, I was able to pray with some of the family who had lost their son, and that made the risk worthwhile.

We also travelled beyond the city to Bucha, where Russian tanks had invaded, bringing devastation in their wake. We walked down one of the streets which I remember watching on the UK news at the start of the invasion, and where homes had been razed to the ground. I listened to the heartbreaking accounts of the atrocities perpetrated by Russian soldiers on the most vulnerable members of society. In some respects, the physical damage can be repaired, but it is hard to see how the deep wounds embedded in the minds of those who lived through these barbaric acts can fully recover. Still, through all of this, these men held fast to their faith in Christ, who knows what it is to carry the deep wounds of suffering. This was the hope I recognised in these men, holding on to Jesus, the only one who can bring any form of healing in the midst of such pain and anguish.

As we returned to Kyiv, there was a clear unease in the city, with a depleted population. The reality hit two days later, having left Kyiv on a high-speed sleeper train, with little sleep, to hear that the city had been hit by more than fifty Russian missiles. Thankfully, the men I had visited were all unharmed. The words of Jesus in the Sermon on the Mount certainly took on a more pertinent meaning, where He says, 'Blessed are those who mourn, for they will be comforted' (Matthew 5:4). I firmly believe that God stands with these men as they mourn significant loss and as they continue to minister among the dispossessed and the hurting, both leaning on and trusting in Christ.

A year after this valuable visit to Ukraine, at the end of July 2023, I and another God's Squad member, from Ireland, had decided to take a further significant 4,000-mile round trip through Europe. We would disembark from the ferry in Holland and travel across Germany, then make two stops in Poland. We would then spend a week between Lithuania, Latvia and Estonia, in order to share fellowship with members of the God's Squad chapters in those countries. Following this, we would take a ferry to Finland, where we would spend the weekend with the chapter there, before riding back across Sweden, Denmark and Germany. We would finally return to Holland, where we would spend some time with the Dutch chapter.

As soon as we docked in Holland, we quickly departed from the ferry, and were immediately hit by torrential rain. This rain was actually going to follow us across Europe, and would not subside until we reached the archipelago islands of Finland.

On our first day we had decided to ride 500 miles just past Poland's border. Here, we would be staying in the home of a

Polish member of God's Squad. Visibility was poor on much of that ride owing to the extreme weather, which made the distance feel even longer. We also discovered that while we were travelling towards Poland, a Dutch member was travelling away and heading back towards Holland. He had been keen to meet up with us on the way, but the logistics of this when travelling in opposite directions seemed unlikely. My companion had actually been receiving messages all day from this member, but hadn't been able to reply, so he could be anywhere along the twelve-hour route. The last message to be picked up asked us if we were anywhere near Magdeburg in Germany. We had actually ridden through Magdeburg hours earlier and were now 100 miles on from that town.

As we approached a petrol station, I felt prompted to stop. So we pulled off the highway to fill up at this extortionately priced garage in Michendorf, which stands just south of Berlin. For the first time that day I picked up my messages, and read one from this Dutch member. I called him just to let him know that we wouldn't be able to meet, while also asking exactly where he was now. We stood in a state of disbelief as he proceeded to tell us that he was actually less than ten minutes from where we were parked, on the opposite side of the highway! There was a burger outlet around the corner, and he knew exactly where this was, having just passed it a couple of minutes before. So, ten minutes later, we were sitting drinking coffee next to our bikes, sharing precious time together on the road, before we finally parted company.

The chances of meeting when travelling vast distances in a foreign country are difficult enough. To ring at the precise moment that both parties have intersected on a 500-mile ride is unimaginable – but this was the reality. Actually, I am convinced that far from a chance call, God had orchestrated this meeting on the road to Poland. In fact, this is just one of many seemingly improbable meetings divinely arranged on the many road trips I have experienced.

Part Six
Maintenance is Key

24

Spiritual Rust and the Right Fuel

It was a warm afternoon back in June 2021 when I headed for a local pub in Shrewsbury that one of the God's Squad members runs. We were meeting there before heading off for a social ride through the Welsh hills. I headed onto the motorway, which I am not overly fond of, but it is the fastest route. On reaching the pub, we relaxed for a while, chatted to some of the locals, and grabbed a coffee. We then headed in the direction of Wales, where we hit the open countryside, with its twists and turns, moving between long, sweeping valleys.

The scenery is picturesque in Wales, with its rolling hills and rugged fields containing numerous flocks of sheep. Traffic is usually light, but there are often bikers enjoying the route. The road leads to a high point, with panoramic views and an isolated café that serves food and drink. This is a popular stop for bikers.

Having enjoyed a pleasant lunch, we returned to our bikes and continued riding for several hours. Some of the roads were relatively straight, but very narrow, and needed to be taken fairly slowly, while others were a little wider and contained several bends that could be taken a little more quickly. If I had known what had been going on with my bike, I may have ambled along these wide-open corners rather than leaning in, along with the group. Nevertheless, we carried on until we reached a small village, where we dismounted and took a stroll before riding back to the pub, where we enjoyed a meal together before saying our goodbyes.

It made sense to ride back together down the motorway. However, I had a nagging feeling that I should take the back roads home, so that was what I did. I hit a ten-mile-an-hour zone, much to my annoyance. But as I slowed down, I thought I could hear a knocking sound from the back wheel. I pulled up and checked, only to find that the rear pulley,[35] which is similar to a cog, had worked loose and was now hanging on by a couple of threads. I couldn't ride the bike any further, but noticed that I was parked right outside a motor vehicle superstore. I pushed the bike into the car park and went in to buy the right size spanner, but ended up buying a set.

I took the panniers off, crouched beside the bike and attempted to tighten the bolts on the pulley. Four of the bolts were shot, as their threads had been completely stripped; one was partially tightened but held, while the other tightened well. It took some time to tighten these two bolts, as there was little room to manoeuvre. I removed the other four bolts from the wheel, and rode the bike for several miles before checking the bolts again. Although it was a slow journey back, I managed to make it home with the rear pulley held on by its threads.

I realise now that I had neglected to add thread lock to the bolts the previous time I had the pulley off. However, not only had the bolts been stripped, but the threads in the wheel were also damaged. While I adapted the wheel temporarily, I did later find a second-hand wheel for this exact model, along with new bolts. This wasn't a bad thing as the wheel hub was badly worn from constant use, and the new wheel was perfect.

I had ridden some dangerous bends that day and thankfully the pulley had held, but the ride home on the motorway would have been my last. The bolts had vibrated themselves out and were millimetres away from hitting the swingarm[36] and jamming

---

[35] The pulley is similar to a cog, attached to the rear wheel, and on most Harley Davidsons there is a belt rather than a chain running to the engine, which rotates the rear wheel.

[36] The swingarm holds the rear wheel and suspension.

the back wheel up. If this had happened on the busy motorway, I would have been thrown off the bike into the path of a car or a lorry, and my chance of survival would have been minimal. I am convinced that God was prompting me to pull off and ride that back road alone, even to the point of me pulling up right outside the shop. It made no human sense to leave the rest of the guys on that motorway, but God knew the consequences of riding together that day.

I have had those feelings before, most of which I have followed – some I haven't, but regretted! One time I had this same sense that I should visit a friend who hadn't been well for a while, and I couldn't get it out of my mind. I almost diverted to visit her, but didn't, and this would have been my last chance to see her before she died later that day. This taught me a lesson, and I try hard now to follow these prompts, which I know come from the Holy Spirit. On this ride, the prompting was strong, and I am convinced that the Holy Spirit was leading me out of danger and saved my life.

Having enjoyed the summer, it was now a cold morning in late 2021 as I was due to ride over to the coast. The roads were thankfully free of the usual stretches of ice, which meant that I could enjoy the bends on this particular stretch of road. However, the bike wasn't steering well through the corners, so as I approached a petrol station, I thought I had better check the steering. Everything seemed OK, until I looked at the forks. I realised that I had picked up a great deal of salt from the road, which was clinging to the chrome inner sections of the forks.[37] I also noticed a greasy substance dripping down the chrome surface. There had obviously been a leak for a while, which I discovered was due to a certain amount of corrosion on the forks themselves caused by the salt on our British roads. Not only do the forks take the shock of the road, but they also affect the steering if there is uneven oil inside the forks themselves.

---

[37] The front forks contain the front wheel suspension.

This was what was upsetting the bike as I took these sharp corners.

One of the most frustrating parts on the bike is this front suspension. The constant compression and decompression which the suspension undergoes during every ride eventually wears the silicon seals that prevent the fork oil from leaking. The seals always seem to give way at the most inconvenient moments. Now one of the forks had begun weeping noticeably, which subsequently increased with every ride. I bit the bullet and bought a set of new fork seals, which I changed over at the weekend. For two days, the fork remained oil free, before beginning to leak once more past this new seal.

We sometimes hit crisis points in life, when initially small issues become greatly magnified. In some ways I had hit a crisis point with the bike as it bled oil from the suspension, completely bypassing its new seal. I tried changing this seal a second time, thinking it may have been faulty, but it still leaked. I examined the fork itself, and noticed some pitting in the slider caused by the large quantities of salt from the roads, but I refused to give up, and tried filling in the pitting with glue, but it still bled. I then tried liquid metal, which worked for a while, but eventually broke loose, leaving this hydraulic bleeding wound haemorrhaging again. Eventually I acknowledged that the patching wasn't going to work, and I bought a new front fork stanchion.

Sometimes we try everything for a quick fix, when really there is an inevitable cost involved. But we need to abandon the things that we know deep down are damaging to us, to receive something new, something better. At times we continue to put sticking plasters on the wounds we carry, so they never heal but remain hidden, and with untreated wounds we can never fully be at peace. Jesus said, 'Come to me, all you who are weary and burdened, and I will give you rest' (Matthew 11:28). At times we need to relinquish those wounds we carry and allow God not to put on another plaster, but to renew our souls, to give us rest. Sometimes we are aware of some deep needs which only God can heal, but we try quick fixes, filling in the cracks, when God wants to bring renewal. There is an honesty that is needed in these situations, and an acknowledgement that we are carrying these things; there needs to be a handing over to God.

There was nothing that could be done for my forks, and I could have continued filling in the pitted surface and wasting time constantly renewing the seals. It was hard to face, but it needed replacing, and once I had come to terms with this, it transformed the ride. Everything was working in the way it was meant to!

Maybe we need to come before God in order to allow Him to bring renewal into our lives, not to make us something different, but to transform us into the person He originally intended us to be. Replacing those forks transformed the whole ride not into something alien, but to its original purpose. I also replaced the stock springs to progressive ones, which actually improved the ride beyond its factory settings; God is able to do this for us too!

I noticed that the salt from the UK roads hadn't just affected the suspension; it had eaten into the mudguards too, causing them to seriously corrode. The difficulty with the mudguards, though, is that they are painted, and this corrosion is not always evident. Around ten years before, I had fitted a perfectly rust-free tank and guards. This was necessitated after a taxi had backed into the bike, radically redesigning the rear fender. I was actually parked in a school car park, and the young people in the back of the cab took great pleasure in jumping out to verbally re-enact the incident. They probably wanted to see how things would play out! Fortunately, the driver was extremely apologetic and was more than happy to cover the cost of the damage. After another ten years on the road, these once pristine mudguards were beginning to show their age. They had been subjected to torrential rain, coarse road grit, and had been sprinkled with more salt than you generally find on your average fish and chips. Needless to say, they had now acquired more than a hint of rust.

I decided to beat out the original mudguards and respray them. They spent a few days in an acid solution, which killed the rust, before I filled the deep indents. I wasn't quite prepared for the extent to which the rust had spread, though, on removing the rear guard. More seriously, the rust had completely eaten through the front fender, producing a sizeable corroded hole. The steady spread of this corrosion had been happening under cover, gradually chipping away at the foundation, turning the healthy metal into something corrosive and destructive. The deceptive nature of the slowly corroding rust as it spread beneath the paint went unnoticed at first, but eventually it was unable to hide itself, and the extent of the damage it had inflicted became apparent. Unfortunately, not all the paint on the frame could be saved, as the corrupting rust had dug too deeply into its integrity, but the rust could certainly be eradicated and fresh paint applied, restoring the frame itself.

In our continuing journey through life, we can be just as affected by the directions we take, by the sometimes poor choices we make, some of which prove corrosive to our soul. The gradual exposure to things which we know are damaging can begin to chip away at our inner integrity. As with the onset of rust on our bikes, we need to recognise when the deceptive and corrosive elements have taken root, and deal with them swiftly before they spread. This was one of the problems in the Old Testament, and one that God was forced to deal with decisively. Here, the Israelites were not only turning to other gods, but were also attempting to incorporate their practices and worship, some of which, like the rust on a bike, threatened to undermine the integrity of the whole people.

In May 2022, I rode over to Ireland with my wife and a few members of God's Squad, where we were attending the joint sixtieth birthday party of two friends and fellow club members. The journey was fairly straightforward until we approached Conway in Wales. We pulled into a petrol station and I filled the tank up. We pulled off, heading for the ferry port in Anglesey, at which the bike began spluttering, spitting and losing power.

We managed to reach the ferry, where we loaded the bikes and settled down for the journey ahead.

On departing the ferry, we pulled into another petrol station, where the bike continued to cause problems. I attempted to start it, but the battery refused to turn the engine over. I was going nowhere.

We contemplated heading straight back onto the ferry, where we would be able to then call a recovery truck to take us home. However, one member from Holland suggested praying, which we should have done earlier. Straight after praying, a man came across to us, asking if everything was alright. We explained that the battery had died, and it was looking like we were going to have to part company. The man had a pair of jump leads in the boot of his car, and he suggested jump-starting the bike, to see if it would at least get us to our destination. It was worth a go, and we would need to get the bike onto the ferry in any case, if we were to make it back to England. He attached the jump leads, I pressed the starter, and the engine turned over.

I ran the bike for a while, before deciding it might be worth heading for our lodgings, hoping for the best. We then set off at some speed, leaving the rest of the group behind, while keeping the revs up. We needed to gauge our approach to roundabouts and traffic lights in order to keep the bike moving, and fortunately there were few of those, and the traffic was also light.

We eventually approached the small Irish village where we were now stopping. We had initially been booked in the place where the celebration was happening, but this had been cancelled at the last minute as it was being used to home refugees. This actually worked out well, as the place we finally ended up staying in was a traditional Irish bed and breakfast, filled with character and history, along with a rear, gated parking area for the bike. The owner was friendly and full of knowledge about the background of the area, as well as the lodgings, which was fascinating to hear.

I made one trip on the bike, and this was to a local tool store, where I purchased a battery charger. I disconnected the battery from the bike and carried the battery up into the hotel room. I attached it to the terminals and left it charging for the next couple of days to make sure we could at least get back to the ferry.

The party itself was full of loud laughter, traditional Irish music and good conversations. It was also an opportunity to enjoy an authentic pint of Guinness which, in my opinion, never really works outside Ireland! Despite the problems with the bike, it was worth persevering to get here.

The journey home was taken in trepidation, at least until we reached the ferry, but we made it back. The bike was running rough, and it took months to work out the actual problem, after trying various fixes, such as new HT leads,[38] purchasing a new battery and changing a fuel line and filter. The solution came after trying all avenues before pulling out the fuel pump itself, which lies in the tank. Having fitted this, along with fuel filters and fuel lines, the problem was rectified. The bike ran like a dream, and it actually felt like a new bike with this pump now supplying the engine with clean fuel. My conclusion was that the fuel in the first petrol station had been bad, and this had finished off the pump which had carried us more than 150,000 miles. The battery had probably died owing to the bike's continual refusal to start because of the bad fuel and a failing pump.

The petrol has the power to animate and bring the vehicle to life when the pump remains clean. In the same way, God is able to bring our faith to life, to keep our hearts pure. He is able to animate our lives, as Jesus said, 'I have come that they may have life, and have it to the full' (John 10:10). It is important that our hearts are able to filter out the stuff that contaminates our souls. On the bike, the filters remove the impurities, but once the tank gets too low, the bits that might have found a way into the tank

---

[38] HT leads carry the electric pulse to the spark plugs.

begin to damage the filters. It is important to continually fill the bike on long journeys, and it isn't good to be running on empty.

Our spiritual lives are a little like that – we can run on empty for a short time, but we need to come to Jesus for renewing, allowing the Holy Spirit to empower us, to fill us, to enable us to continue on our faith journey. We can make choices to fill our lives with the things that give us peace and joy, providing us with real freedom.

The right petrol allows the bike to reach its full potential, but it needs to be drawn from the right source. When Jesus left the disciples after the resurrection, He told them to wait in Jerusalem for the gift of the Holy Spirit, saying, 'I am going to send you what my Father has promised; but stay in the city until you have been clothed with power from on high' (Luke 24:49). This word for 'power' in Greek – *dunamis* – is where we get our word for dynamite. The petrol in the tank doesn't remain passive, doesn't just flow into the engine; it is pumped under pressure, it explodes into life as it powers these great pistons. Our walk with God isn't passive either, and when we allow the explosive power of the Holy Spirit to bring life to our souls, our ride with God on this sometimes unpredictable and winding road proves to be a powerful journey. Life with God is certainly never boring.

25
Maintenance Manuals and Freedom to Breathe

One of the most necessary items that allows the Harley to function never touches the bike itself. Without it, though, bolts can sheer in two and whole engines can be destroyed – even the rider can have their life extinguished without its safeguards. Whether the bike is taken to a Harley Davidson specialist or worked on at home, the manual makes it safe, reveals the solutions to potential damage and is a guide for appropriate maintenance. It is the maker's instructions, the instructions of the one who created the heart of the bike, and who tells us how to look after it. When things go wrong, it becomes a guide to get us out of trouble; when the bike is damaged, it becomes a manual helping us to restore it. We are only able to guess how to fix certain parts, or to maintain elements of the bike, before coming unstuck.

There is no shame in going back to the basics, back to the maker, to remind us why we follow certain routines on the bike, just as we follow certain routines in our faith walk, which need to be in line with our Maker's instructions – in line with the Bible.

I am referring to my own bike manual more regularly, which is why despite the exhaust falling off some time ago, along with a heat shield and the drive belt,[39] the bike is in good working order. In reality, it isn't highly polished, and it bears the scars of long rides and carries the wounds inflicted by winter salt. But fundamentally it is sound.

For some of us, we may physically or emotionally carry scars, the wounds of a long, hard journey through life's sometimes long winters. Often suffering is part and parcel of the Christian walk; it certainly was for Jesus. But this is where we need to find comfort from our spiritual manual, from the Bible, to correct parts of our life that may be damaging or unhealthy, to allow Christ to speak to us through the pages, as He is present with us through the Holy Spirit.

Life on a Harley Davidson is not always smooth. The engine vibrates, the wheels find more bumps than a car, turning the bike takes effort and changing a tyre is hard work. A moped would be easier, an electric bike would be smoother and a limousine would be more comfortable! Riding a Harley, though, is not designed to be easy all the time; it isn't designed to be so smooth you can't feel the road.

Riding a Harley is, in my opinion, unmatched; it has character, it has tones that resonate with unique beauty. Taking to the roads brings joy to the soul, but at times it can be hard – when the rain comes or the snow falls, when the road isn't pleasant; when the brakes complain, or the tyres slip, or the fingertips feel the pain of a freezing wind. But the journey remains worth the pain, worth the suffering, worth the work. When the salt bites into the frame and the grime corrodes its veins, it is still worth it.

The manual doesn't prevent the corrosion, doesn't prevent the suffering, but it shows us how to live with it, shows us how to deal with it. The maker has given us the manual for life and the resources to bring us through, both on our bikes and in our faith walk. Just as the Harley manual helps us to follow the

---

[39] The heat shields cover the exhausts and give some protection from serious burns from the hot exhausts.

maker's instructions, so the Bible allows us to follow our Maker's instructions. Once we get this right, we are ready once more for our continued journeys through the excitement of life's twists, turns and surprises, but always riding with God at our side.

While maintaining our bikes is crucial, maintaining ourselves with adequate riding gear is just as important, as we too are prone to malfunction and operator error. I was heading on a long journey to Europe during the winter of 2022 and was aware that I needed a little more warmth for riding on this occasion.

One of the biggest problems to overcome on a motorcycle is windchill, making freezing temperatures even more biting. Several of my mates now have windscreens fitted, which helps eradicate this, but I find them constrictive and can't bring myself to fit one on my Harley. I ride all year round, and conditions can include rain, snow or sub-zero temperatures. Without the right gear, a long ride can steadily bring on the effects of hypothermia, which can be fatal.

I hate buying new riding gear, but I have found a thick woollen jumper is one of the most useful items you can own for riding in sub-zero conditions, or for emergency use. After fifteen years, though, my travelling jumper isn't what it used to be, with more holes in it than the average political speech. I finally decided to order a replacement, while the old one still sits permanently in my panniers. Sizing is something of a difficult art, so when this new riding jumper arrived, it was massively oversized, and I was discouraged from wearing it by my wife, particularly outside the confines of the house. However, I came up with a plan to make it fit, which was to ask my wife to slightly shrink it in the washing machine. I had complete confidence, as she has been able to shrink jumpers in the past without me even needing to ask.

The plan worked all too well, and on bringing it out, it had the consistency of carpet. It would only just fit my young grandson, and may have been useful as a leg warmer, if I only had a pair. Needless to say, I ordered a smaller size, which has saved me from getting hypothermia on many a ride in the winter months.

I guess many of us can feel like this jumper, constricted, limited and sometimes almost hardened by our experiences. The world is changing, with pressure from all sides, leaving us feeling, at times, as if we are being forced into a straightjacket. It feels for some as if our world is shrinking rapidly, as with my jumper.

I know there are no easy answers, and no quick fixes, but I know that God is able to renew a once constricted life, bringing comfort and softening hardened experiences. I am reminded of the pastoral words of the apostle Peter: 'Cast all your anxiety on him because he cares for you' (1 Peter 5:7). I believe as we do this, the feelings of suffocation will ease, and we will feel the freedom to breathe.

Part Seven
Beyond the Church

26
The Heart of the Matter

It was a cold October morning in 2018 when an old friend from up north was visiting. We had met in Morecambe many years before and shared a flat there, after he had let me sleep in the boot of his Ford Escort for a week. This was in the early eighties, when crashing out in various places was not uncommon.

I decided to take him to our local cathedral on this very cold day, which was even colder in the cathedral. My friend is fairly affluent, and lives a slightly different lifestyle to me, enjoying spending time at his local and exclusive golf club, and all that comes with that life. So a cultured walk around the cathedral before grabbing a real ale appealed to him.

As we walked along the aisle of the cathedral, we heard what could only be described as a loud yelp, which echoed from one side of the cathedral to the other, with visitors looking around to see what the problem was.

This yelp, which was aimed at me, consisted of the words, 'Get your hat off!' While I had a few words to say about this, my friend was absolutely incensed. He rightly pointed out that a gentleman in formal wear had walked by just prior to us, with not a word about this man's flat cap. He also said it was highly disrespectful, yelling across a building, rather than coming up and having a quiet word.

The reality was that in my slightly worn leather jacket, with my beanie hat on, I didn't look as respectable as the man with the formal clothing. Ironically, at that time, I had just been ordained in this very cathedral, wearing different attire, with very different attitudes from the officials there. As has been the case several times, particularly when biking, a judgement call had been made based on outward appearance that would have been very different if I had been wearing my clerical collar. The perceived respectability, based on a religiosity, was more important than having the opportunity to take a friend with no faith into a place of Christian worship.

This reminded me of the way Jesus challenged the hypocrisy within the religious structures, of those who were so concerned about the self-constructed external regulations that they had neglected the important inner reality. Jesus talked about ceremonial washing of hands, or even food that can cause a bad stomach, asserting that these cannot damage the significant inner integrity. What comes out of a person's heart, as Jesus says, is what damages, and these are the symptoms of a different kind of sickness, not physical but spiritual.[40]

In reality, food in itself has no effect on our moral or spiritual state, neither does the way we dress, what we wear, including leather cut-offs, tattoos or piercings. Instead, as Jesus says, it is what comes from our *heart* that damages our inner integrity. We may need to look beyond a person's outward appearance to see the individual, to discern their heart, which in the end is the most important thing.

While being judged on the way we look is not good, one time I deserved to be judged was shortly after my ordination in November 2018. I was conducting one of my first funerals for a local vicar, and it was a big occasion. It was also one of the biggest learning curves in my ministry. It is good to make mistakes in the presence of small numbers, or among a friendly congregation. This is why it is sometimes good for preachers, as they present their first sermons, to do so when not too many people are present, such as at a midweek service. However, I

---

[40] Matthew 15:1-20.

seldom do things by halves, and this was the biggest funeral I had attended, let alone presided at.

The day for me began on Friday morning, when I settled down to have breakfast and go through the Order of Service for the last time. It was 11am and the funeral didn't begin until 1pm, so I had plenty of time, or so I thought!

As I picked up my coffee mug, the phone rang. 'Where are you? The coach has been here for ten minutes and they are waiting outside.'

I nearly spat my coffee all over the lounge table. The coach they were referring to was a large, glass-encased, horse-drawn carriage, pulled by two elegant steeds. As the reality hit, that I had misread the timings as 1:00 instead of 11:00, I quickly grabbed my things, climbed on the Harley and tore across town to the church where the funeral was being held. As I walked in at 11.30am, I could feel the animosity moving through the air, emanating from a completely packed congregation. I disappeared into a side room, changed out of my leathers into my clerical robes and immediately began the funeral.

Thankfully the service ran smoothly, with hostilities dying down slightly as people exited, and the coach made its way to the cemetery. I should have learned my lesson, having been late in the first place. However, the cemetery was some distance away and the horses were travelling slowly. I decided that I had time for a quick coffee before I left for the cemetery, and I would still have plenty of time to beat the carriage. I certainly needed a strong, sweet coffee.

After drinking my coffee, I climbed once more onto the bike, pulled out of the church car park and attempted to cross the road, through the busy rush-hour traffic. I slowly pulled out towards the middle of the road, and turned the handlebars. The bars faced one way, while the front wheel moved in the opposite direction. The bike appeared to slip on to its side in slow motion, clipping a car and leaving me lying with this heavy Harley on top of me.

Three men in hoodies approached me, and I wasn't sure at that point what their intentions were; nothing would have surprised me after these two disasters. Thankfully, though, they helped lift the bike off me, asking if I was alright.

I had barely stood up as blood began to drip from my knee down my ripped jeans onto the ground. I tried frantically to start the bike, but it refused. One of the men told me that he was going to call for an ambulance. I told him I was on my way to a funeral, to which he said, 'You're going nowhere in that condition.' What had actually happened was that a large oil slick was sitting right in the middle of the road where I had turned, and my front wheel had hit this and lost traction, taking the bike over. It had landed on my knee, which was now swollen, painful and dripping with blood. The fall had obviously flooded the engine, which is why it refused to start. The car I had clipped was long gone by now. I climbed on the bike and tried starting it again.

To my relief, the engine turned over, and I rode through the now stationary traffic, through town and onto the dual carriageway that led to the cemetery. I rode a little faster than I would have liked, passing a few cars which were most likely also heading for the cemetery. I pulled back the throttle as I headed for the roundabout that would lead me back down the carriageway in the opposite direction, to the cemetery. As I sped towards the roundabout, the exhaust backfired just as I passed a coach and horses. Harleys are loud machines, and ordinarily when passing horses, I slow right down or turn off the engine. However, in my haste I only noticed them once I had overtaken them.

I reached the cemetery, changed into my clerical robes next to the bike, with bloodstained jeans, and waited for the carriage to arrive. I then walked across to find an irate woman, who was trying to calm the horses, telling people how a Harley had roared past and exploded at some speed, frightening them. Unwisely, I admitted that it was me who had ridden past, and apologised, explaining that I had come off the bike on the way, which was why I had ridden so quickly. However, I received little sympathy from the woman. In fact, no one really wanted to talk to me after I admitted this, and I was imagining a final pile-up as the horses bolted, with cars overturned and newsreaders recounting the story. Fortunately, the woman managed to control the horses, and they arrived in one piece.

The final ceremony went ahead, and I joined them for the wake afterwards. I can't say I felt particularly welcome, though a lady did fetch me some food. She also asked me if I had been at the funeral, and how I knew the deceased person. I told her that I was the vicar who had conducted the funeral, and she said she hadn't recognised me with my biker gear on. This certainly could have been a blessing in that hostile environment. I didn't stay long… but was still glad I went.

I have to say, while this was not my finest hour, it is comforting to know that in our failings, God does not write us off. I was actually devastated for some time over this, and several apologies needed to be expressed, both by me and by the vicar of the church. I might at this point have decided not to conduct any more funeral services, but was relieved this wasn't my decision.

The important thing is to learn from our mistakes and to do things differently in future. I have subsequently conducted many funerals, and am glad to have had the opportunity to bring comfort and support in times of deep need. I have also been grateful for the kind words I have often been sent by the families who have been particularly grateful for this support.

I am reminded of the apostle Peter here, who continually made some big mistakes as he walked with Jesus – his biggest being his denial of Jesus, which tore him apart.[41] However, Jesus forgave him, and gave him another chance. Peter learned from his mistakes and became the leader of those early disciples.

---

[41] Luke 22:56-62

So God never writes us off when we are willing to learn from our mistakes, and sometimes our mistakes change us for the better. This has certainly been my experience!

27
Sharing Grace

In 2021 I rode to Llandudno, which is a Victorian seaside resort in Wales. Llandudno is a great place to visit, and it has a track that runs up the adjacent mountain and down towards the sea, before tracing the coast on a one-way route around the base of the mountainside. I often ride over on my own, and stop for the night in a local and extremely cheap hotel room. I also ring my wife while I am there, usually at night, while walking by the sea.

This occasion was no exception, as I decided to wander to the end of a small, narrow jetty that leads out to sea. As I stood chatting, staring into the water, I heard footsteps behind me, and turned to see who it was. It was in fact a man who had not noticed me in the dark, and who was a little shocked to find me at the end of the jetty, apparently talking to myself, as I stared into the deep water ahead. I don't know if he was concerned that I was going to throw myself in, but he looked more than a little anxious.

I said, 'I have just been talking to my wife,' to which he replied, 'I'm really sorry.'

I said, 'She's gone now, though,' to which he again replied in a sympathetic manner, 'That must be really difficult for you.'

I thought, 'It's not that difficult ending a phone conversation with my wife.' Then, sensing he might have got hold of the wrong end of the stick, I said, 'No, I was just talking to her on the phone, but now she's gone.'

At this he backed up slowly and made his way swiftly across the sand.

It is easy to make assumptions before getting the whole story. We often do this with the Bible, taking parts out of context, without reading the whole section. We can get a wrong understanding of who God is, or read into the gospel what we want to hear. The pendulum has swung in two directions in the past, where Christians have preached a harsh gospel of judgement at the expense of grace, or they have preached a liberal gospel of grace without repentance, belief or a call to live differently.

When John wrote in his Gospel, 'For God so loved the world that he gave his one and only Son,' it demonstrated God's immense love for us. However, John then continues, 'that whoever believes in him shall not perish but have eternal life' (John 3:16), and the conditions emerge, which are to actually believe in Him. In fact, John continues, 'For God did not send his Son into the world to condemn the world, but to save the world through him' (John 3:17), which is the good news. However, if we stop there, we miss the equally important warning that 'Whoever believes in him is not condemned, but whoever does not believe stands condemned already because they have not believed in the name of God's one and only Son' (John 3:18).

Love is God's incentive, Jesus' death is the solution and belief is the key, whereas disbelief is leaving the key on the table. There are consequences, but God's desire is for us to believe, to be saved. If we read only that 'God so loved the world that he gave his one and only Son', we fail to get the whole picture, just like the man on the jetty. God loves us, but we need to respond to that love, and if we read on in this section of John, we find that we need to repent and to live differently in response to God's amazing grace.

Another ride through England in 2022 took me to Morecambe, where I had a couple of days to spare. While Morecambe isn't usually the most sought-after destination, it does have several surrounding villages that have a great deal of character and history. Morecambe also holds some good memories for me, as I once shared a flat there with a friend, as I mentioned earlier, and it was the place where I met my wife. I also often stop over when I ride to Glasgow to visit my son, as it gives me a break and is roughly a halfway point.

On this particular day, the ride had been pleasant with not too many traffic jams, and the weather was reasonable. I was spending the night in Morecambe in a cheap seafront hotel, intending to visit some of the characteristic villages in that area. I had a wander along the seafront, stopped off at a local café, finding a table overlooking the sea, and had some lunch.

After lunch, I had a ride over to visit an ancient church, and spent some time wandering around an ancient burial ground that had been there long before the church. This burial ground contains stone-built tombs that it is possible to enter, and was built on a mound, with great bird's-eye views of the sea.

On the way back, I rode along what looks like an alien landscape, with a narrow, raised track leading across a mud flat, where the sea creates all manner of weird and wonderful patterns. The track can be dangerous, as it leads across the immense mud-filled landscape. Here, the sea often covers the track with wet mud and slime, as the tide comes in. At one point I nearly lost the traction on the back tyre, which would have been disastrous, as this raised track has no barriers to prevent the numerous vehicles from slipping into the deep mud, and the bike would have swiftly disappeared, along with myself. I took it a little slower after that near miss.

The other unique feature of these mud flats is that they disappear as the tide comes in, and it comes in quickly. I had reached the beach on the far side of the track, and noticed the sea coming in at pace. I climbed back on the bike and began steadily returning along this track. However, the sea was beating me to the other side. I could now not see the surface, at points, as the sea began to cover the track. I barely made it, as I rode through the shallow water on this potential death trap. As I looked back, having climbed up an incline, there was no sign of either track or mud flats, but only the wide-open sea lapping onto the beach. There are several treacherous areas in Morecambe, and it was not so long ago that cockle pickers lost their lives as they were rapidly cut off from the shore.[42]

Having had more than enough adventures for the day, I decided to visit a pub in the evening. The pub, the oldest in Morecambe, had been famous for smugglers, and still has a tunnel that leads to the sea. It has lots of character, and has remained open after weathering the pandemic. I decided to wander down for a quick pint of real ale, which the pub has a good reputation for. The tables were taken, but some people asked me if I wanted to share theirs, which I did. I told them that I was up from Leicester, visiting for the weekend, and they told me that they knew it very well. Then they asked me what I did. I foolishly mentioned that I was a vicar.

The pub soon came alive. I ordered another pint of ale which I stood at the bar with, as I chatted with the regulars. We talked a little about bikes, reminiscing about the old motorcycle shop that used to exist round the corner and where I bought a motorcycle nearly forty years before. We chatted about the holiday camp where I had met my wife, and one of the guys shared that he had worked there too.

Someone then called out loudly, 'You're never a vicar!' Word had obviously got around. A conversation then broke out across the whole bar debating whether I was or wasn't actually a vicar, which was quite surreal. The person who had been talking to me earlier then asked me if God could really forgive them. I obviously answered, 'Yes!' We then had a conversation about forgiveness, and why Jesus had died, with the others at the bar joining in. Then the person I'd been talking with asked me to pray with them, which I did.

---

[42] www.bbc.co.uk/news/uk-england-lancashire-25986388 (accessed 5th October 2023).

As I began to pray, in the middle of this pub, the person proceeded to fall sideways, exactly the way a tree falls in a forest. I knelt down and finished praying, thinking maybe the Spirit was at work. Someone else mentioned that this person fell over all the time, and eventually they got up. I think this was one of the most unusual faith conversations I have ever had.

At times I am astonished by fascinating situations like this that I have been led into, the numerous opportunities I have been given to share my own faith journey, or the privilege of sharing life on the road with valued friends, faithful companions and precious brothers. This journey has taken me down some dark valleys, but it has also taken me into some real mountaintop experiences, which often seem to go hand in hand.

Through all of this, God has been faithful as He has journeyed with me on this amazing road, with twists and turns, steep climbs and gentle slopes, cold, numbing winds and warm summer breezes.

The journey continues, but not alone, never alone, as Jesus rides beside.